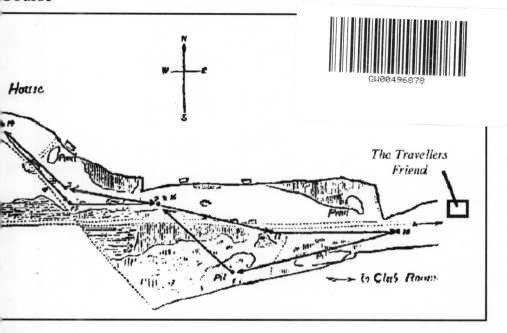

eyed 1874, Revised 1933)

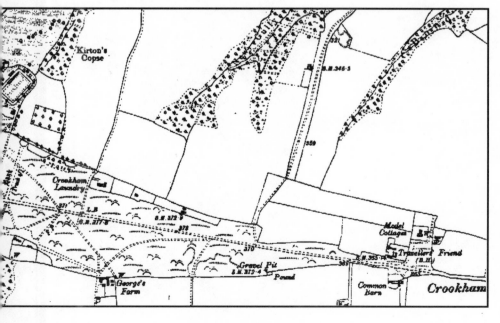

R.Dashwood Fowler R.N.
The co-founder of Crookham

The Golf Courses of Newbury and Crookham

1873 - 1995

by

Brian Bowness

Grant and Hobbs, Worcestershire 1996

ISBN 0 907186 70 X

Typeset and printed by Bigwood & Staple
Bridgwater, Somerset, England

Published in a limited edition of 750 copies
by Grant and Hobbs
The Coach House, Cutnall Green,
Droitwich, Worcestershire WR9 0PQ

The Golf Courses of
Newbury and Crookham
1873 - 1995

Published in a limited edition of 750 copies
of which the first 45 copies are The Subscribers Edition

Copy No: **494.**

Grant and Hobbs, Worcestershire 1996

Contents

		Page
Acknowledgments		viii
Introduction		x
Part I	Crookham Golf Club	1
1	*The Early Years 1873-1880*	3
2	*The Second Phase 1891-1914*	22
3	*Between the Wars 1920-1930*	33
4	*The Final Years 1930-1946*	45
Part II	Newbury District Golf Club	57
5	*The Founding 1923-1930*	59
6	*Pre War Years 1931-1939*	80
7	*Wartime and After 1939-1946*	89
Part III	Newbury & Crookham Golf Club	101
8	*The Amalgamation 1946-1962*	103
9	*The Course and Clubhouse 1963-1973*	114
10	*The Evolution of the Course 1923-1995*	126
11	*Recent Years 1974-1995*	137
12	*The Roll of Honour*	152
13	*Appendix*	171

Acknowledgments

There are many people to thank for their assistance throughout this project.

From the start, in 1991, renowned historians, John Behrend, Alick Watt, David Stirk and John Goodban were generous with their encouragement and help.

When researching our founder members, I pestered Robert Smart, at St Andrews University, Gordon Christie, also of St Andrews, Peter Lewis at the British Golf Museum, the Rev. Brian Harris at the rectory, Great Casterton, Mrs Dorothy Smallwood of Brimpton and Ian Dashwood Moir, great grandson of Capt. R. Dashwood Fowler. They all provided clues and leads that led me to my goal.

Mrs Vi Fielding, a kind lady in her 80s, provided me with vital information regarding the Rev. J. Scott Ramsay. She recalls him as a very gentle man who, when she was between six and 12 years old, bounced her on his knee when he lodged with her maiden aunts in Hoylake during the last six years of his life. She directed me to his overgrown grave in a closed cemetery in Hoylake, where the broken headstone gives evidence of his life in the service of the church.

Only two people replied to my various appeals for news and information about Crookham. Charlie Smith of Thatcham provided valuable photographs of Wally Clinch and The Volunteer Inn. He recalled spending many hours in Clinch's workshop as a boy, and proudly tells how Clinch made him a cut-down set of clubs "of his own". Bill Tibble of Thatcham provided the old photograph of The Travellers' Friend.

It was impossible to write any article concerning life after 1923 that did not require help and guidance from Jack Hughes, Len Moore and Frank Barton.

Thanks also to June Hearsey, Amanda Fisher and Anne Thomas for various degrees of help and patience.

Generous treatment was also received from Berkshire County Council, St Andrews University and Library, Wimbledon Museum, Burlington Galleries, West Publications, the Royal & Ancient, the Ministry of Defence, *The Field* and many others.

My good friend, Allan Mercado, has willingly provided photographs. Jim Hamilton and Paul Sievers produced photographs of the course, and Vince Taylor the sketches.

I cannot over-emphasise the value of the assistance given by the *Newbury Weekly News* through its editor, Lou Cummins. I have been allowed unlimited access to their library, which has been the dominant source of the facts and commentaries reproduced in the book.

In four years I have scanned over 5,000 copies of the paper in an estimated 250 hours, and all in someone else's office! The *Newbury Weekly News* librarian, Jenny Jackson, has been the soul of patience and kindness. Paul Jordan of the *Newbury Weekly News* also provided valuable practical help in compiling course photographs and drawings, as did Ray Clarke with proof reading.

Lou Cummins, a keen Newbury & Crookham member, kindly read through each section as it was completed, giving professional and friendly advice and, above all, giving me the confidence to carry it through.

When we were faced with converting our text onto a different disc, Maggie Carr came to our rescue, and we owe her our thanks.

Thanks too, to my wife Gill who has given me encouragement all the way.

I must above all thank the club committee for having confidence in me and backing the venture from the start.

The final paragraph which Jacquie Wailes will type for this book, is dedicated to conveying my thanks to her for the marathon job she has performed for me and for the club. Neither of us visualised the project would take four years, or would we have started? I struggle to adequately express my thanks to her for her remarkable tolerance and patience. She has never complained and has only ever pretended to be happy doing the job for which she so foolishly volunteered.

Brian Bowness

Introduction

On my first visit to Newbury & Crookham Golf Club in 1962, I parked my car facing across the first fairway. A familiar figure, Ted Howard, walked across the fairway towards me, swinging a club through the grass with his right hand, and in doing so, sweetly chipped a stone through my windscreen.

After becoming a member, if I gave any thought to the name of the club at all, I presumed "Crookham" was included because the course was in that vicinity, and wondered why "Greenham" didn't warrant a mention. Eventually I became vaguely aware of the origin of the "Crookham" factor, but with no more interest than any other member, and no desire to pursue the subject.

I later became a collector of antique sporting items, at first from every sport, but later concentrating only on golf. In 1990 I joined the British Golf Collectors Society, and rapidly learned more of the history of the game.

The man who proposed my membership was Alick Watt, one of the country's leading authorities on golf history, particularly on golf clubs and their makers, and a well known writer on the subject. Through Alick, and the Society, I found a source of knowledge and information which inspired me. Visits to such places as Westward Ho!, St. Andrews, Hoylake and other historic courses awakened the desire for more knowledge, and apart from collecting clubs, balls and other items, I gradually acquired a golf library which includes several golf club histories.

Soon I realised that we were members of a club which, through its early connection with Crookham, had a story to tell.

As Crookham was one of the first courses in England, the name, I felt, should be perpetuated so that we, and golf historians would never forget it.

Some of what is written will please the golf historian, but most of this story is put together for the members, so that they can realise what a proud heritage we all have.

Visualise the scenes at the first clubhouse, The Traveller's Friend, in 1873; there are horse carriages arriving, filling the forecourt. Ladies in long, full dresses, gentlemen with clubs and baggage hurrying into the public house, not to change into very different clothes (it was natural to play golf at that time in normal day clothes), but for some to don that one vital item that completes the picture – the red coat.

Each player would bring, or be allocated, a caddie who would carry the clubs loose under one arm.

In an area less than one mile past the present clubhouse in Burys Bank Road and stretching for three miles towards Brimpton, mostly now within the fencing of Greenham Common Airbase, there were fairways of lush grass, edged by heather and bushes. There were ponds and trees, but no sand. Bunkers at that time were a purely natural development on links courses caused mostly by sheep huddling for shelter from winds from the sea. Greenkeepers and course architects were not yet so devious as to manufacture them.

With no cars, no aeroplanes, and a widespread community, it must have been a wonderful, peaceful place. What leisurely golf they would have enjoyed. How different from the busy fairways of today.

It was the pioneers of Crookham Golf Club who brought the game to Newbury. It was they who aroused the curiosity of local people which eventually led to the opening of the Newbury District Club in 1923, the two clubs running alongside each other until the Second World War.

In the minute books of this period I found the reference to the merger of the two clubs, although the Crookham course had by then (March 4th 1946) disappeared.

A vital moment in our history is the proposal by Mr Horace de Vere Buckingham that the name of the joint club should be "Newbury and Crookham Golf Club".

There were few remaining Crookham members and they had little to offer the merger, but how fortunate that the committee of that time had the wisdom and generosity to acknowledge, and perpetuate, the memory of Crookham.

Had Crookham Golf Club survived it would stand in seventh place in the table of the oldest clubs in England. This fact could be challenged because, occasionally, 1872 is quoted as the opening year of the club, but this probably refers to the date of its conception rather than its actual opening.

Those known to have preceded Crookham are: Royal Blackheath (1608), Old Manchester (1817 – 9 holes), London Scottish (1864 – Royal Wimbledon), Royal North Devon (1864 – Westward Ho!), Royal Liverpool (1869) and Alnmouth (1869).

"…….thence sprang up golf all over England, by seaside links and on deplorable commons where the hazards are whins and 'the green' is a food deep in vegetation".
Badminton Library – Golf, 1890 Andrew Lang

Part I

Crookham Golf Club

The first Crookham clubhouse

1

The Early Years 1873 – 1880

The most vivid way to describe the opening years of Crookham Golf Club, is to reproduce the reports as they appeared in *The Field* magazine.

In July 1873 the *Newbury Weekly News* reproduced an article from *The Field*, which first described play, and visitors to the course.

The Field April 19th 1873

Lovers of the game of golf are doubtless desirous that it should spread in this country and become as popular as it is in the Land o'Cakes; they will therefore be interested in the announcement that it has been established in Berkshire.

The links are on Crookham Common, the fine site of the encampment of 1,500 men on their march to Salisbury Plain last year, which is distant from Newbury about four miles, and from the Thatcham Station a little more than a mile.

Eighteen holes are obtained in a course of nearly four miles, and plenty of hazards (in the absence of sand and bunkers) present themselves in the shape of gorse and heather. The putting greens are capable of improvement which will without doubt be soon effected by the club which is about to be established. Four foursomes were played at the same time yesterday.

The Field July 5th 1873

Golf in Berkshire

A few weeks back we briefly mentioned the introduction of the game into another district, where it had never previously been played. Crookham Heath or Common, situated on the southern border of Berkshire, near Newbury and the site of a large encampment during the last autumn manoeuvres, is this time the scene of the sport, and affords one of the finest golfing grounds that could be found in this country. The heath is about four miles in length, and a mile or mile and a half in width, and throughout its course is as level, comparatively speaking, as a billiard table. This, however, is not necessarily an advantage in the eyes of golfers, who like to encounter the difficulties of a somewhat broken ground; but Crookham Heath presents the necessary "hazards" in frequent clumps of gorse and patches of heather, while at one spot there is an avenue of moderate-sized trees, which have to be cleared by the golfer in striking off. The situation of the common is high, commanding views of the hills of Hampshire, Berkshire and adjacent counties, from which the breezes sweep freely over the heath, so that a more pleasant and suitable spot could hardly be found for this health-giving recreation.

The golfing links commence at the farther end of the common from Newbury, near the Thatcham Station of the Reading and Hungerford Branch of the Great Western

Railway. At an inn known as "Traveller's Friend" on the eastern extremity of the common, a club-room has been obtained for the use of members, and near this house is the starting point of the links. The entire distance covered by the eighteen holes into which the links are as usual divided, is about four miles out and home, and the ground traversed skirts the main road across the common from Aldermaston to Newbury.

The Crookham Golf Club numbers at present about twenty members, including most of the gentry whose seats are in the immediate locality. To the honorary secretary, Captain Fowler R.N., belongs the credit of initiating golf at Crookham, the idea of the suitability of the heath for the game having occurred to him, as he informed us, when he was playing at Westward Ho! Mr. Ramsay, a gentleman formerly known on St Andrews links, is also one of the members and founders of the club. Its practice days are usually Monday and Friday in each week, but occasionally other days are set apart for play, as circumstances may require. Crookham Heath has already been visited by some of our golfers from town, and from the Devonshire head-quarters of golf in England; and a few days back Mr Gossett, the celebrated player of the Royal North Devon tried his skill upon the links, and expressed a very favourable opinion of its capabilities. The day of our visit to Crookham was somewhat unfavourable, a very wet morning having precluded the likelihood of the presence of any golfers on the ground; but in the after part of the day we found Capt. Fowler and Mr Ramsay engaged in practice, with the indifference to weather which characterises all true golfers. As the club becomes more widely known, we have no doubt the number of its members will greatly increase, and that the Crookham links will rank hereafter among the most prominent in the kingdom.

The following are particulars of the play of the last few days: on Friday, the 27th, Gen. Wilson, Gen. Vassal, and Mr Gossett, of the Westward-Ho! Club, came from London and played a foursome with Mr Thackwell. The generals had to return by an early train, but Mr Gossett remained, and had a good match with the Rev. J. Scott Ramsay, of the Crookham Club.

On Wednesday, July 2nd, Col. Kennard, Messrs Glennie, Baldwin, McCandlish, and Mercer came down by train, accompanied by Bob Kirk, the professional, and the following games were played: A foursome, Col. Kennard and Mr Mercer v. Mr Baldwin and the Rev. J. Scott Ramsay, won by the latter by six up and five to play; they also won the bye by two holes. Foursome, Messrs. Glennie and McCandlish v. Capt. Dashwood Fowler and Bob Kirk, won by the former by three holes; a short game of 12 holes was also won by the same gentlemen. Foursome, Col. Kennard and Rev. J.S. Ramsay v. Mr Baldwin and Mr Mercer, 10 holes, won by the former by three up and two to play; they also won the bye. Mr Baldwin had a match with the Rev. J.S. Ramsay, which he won by two up and one to play.

On the latter day the club was poorly represented, owing to its not being a club day, the majority of members being engaged to a large garden party in the neighbourhood. There were, however, several carriages on the ground full of ladies, and others walked with the players watching the game with much interest. The day was very fine, and the glorious view of the Hampshire hills, with the beautiful woods of Highclere Castle (Lord Carnarvon's), was rendered still more enjoyable by the exhilarating air of the common.

The visitors named in these extracts are significant figures in the history of golf, for they, and others like them, take considerable credit for the spread of golf in their lifetime.

It would have been a great boost to the Crookham Club to have these gentlemen travel from Blackheath to sample its course. With so few courses outside Scotland, much travelling, mostly by rail, was necessary to exchange visits and hospitality. Each club hosted "competitions", either team events or, as in the case of Crookham the following year, an "Open". Matches were also favoured, in particular between the professionals upon which there would be betting and side stakes.

From the book of *The History of Royal Blackheath* (Stirk and Henderson) the following information has been extracted:

George Glennie (1818-1886)

He became a member of Blackheath in 1853, winning the Spring Medal in 1854, and his victories in this, the Summer Medal and the Bombay Medal, three major competitions at Blackheath, numbered 14.

He also won the Club Gold Medal at Westward Ho! three times, and the King William IV Gold Medal of the Royal & Ancient in 1855 with a score of 88 which went unbeaten until improved by Horace Hutchinson. He also won the Royal & Ancient Silver Medal in 1851.

He was one of the strongest players in the country, but unfortunately had no chance to prove his worth as national championships began too late for him.

Representing Blackheath with Captain J. C. Stewart of the 72nd Highlanders, they won the Grand Tournament at St Andrews in 1857. This was a foursomes tournament and Blackheath elected them both life members on the strength of their win.

Glennie was captain of Blackheath in 1862 and 1863, and was elected secretary and treasurer in 1868, duties he performed until his death.

In 1881 Blackheath honoured Glennie by having the George Glennie Medal struck. Two medals were made, one being sent to the Royal & Ancient for annual competition, and one for Blackheath. Both are still played for today.

Lieutenant Colonel E.H. Kennard (1836-1912)

Born in Hackney, Kennard was elected a member of Blackheath Golf Club in 1852, aged 16.

He subsequently won all of Blackheath's major scratch competitions, also winning their Spring Medal on six occasions, 30 years separating the first and last victory.

He graduated from Oxford in 1858, joining the Queen's Own 7th Regiment of Light Dragoons. In 1874/5 he was MP for Lymington.

Kennard became a member of Royal North Devon (Westward Ho!) and was elected president in 1873. In 1870 he became a founder member of Royal Liverpool and was captain in 1872 and 1873. In 1875 he joined Wimbledon Golf Club, being captain in 1882. In 1868 he became a Royal & Ancient member. He was a founder member of Royal St George's and later, captain. He was made captain of Blackheath in 1875, and became a member at Crookham in the same year.

Kennard became a field marshal in 1894.

The illustrations paint a wonderful picture of the likely scenes at Crookham in 1873. With Colonel Kennard (right), the caddie can be seen placing the ball on a mound of earth for a tee shot. The man, shown between Col. Kennard and his caddie, is another of the visitors, W.McCandlish.

In the picture of Glennie (left), his caddie 'Dick' Steer is also seen carrying the clubs and McCandlish is again in the picture, extreme right. The balls used throughout the period from 1848 to 1898 were the "gutty". By 1873 the gutty ball had been developed to a stage that was to prevail until the rubber core ball was invented in 1898.

Robert Kirk (1845-1886)

Was appointed professional of Royal Blackheath in 1868, coming from St Andrews, where he regularly caddied for Old Tom Morris. He was a good golfer and clubmaker. In 1865 he was third in the Open Championship, and in 1870 was runner-up to Tom Morris Jnr. (This was Morris's third successive win which gave him "the Belt" outright). Kirk was also runner up in 1878. He was an enigmatic character and remained with Blackheath until 1876 and was replaced by the Crookham professional Thomas Manzie. He then returned to St Andrews.

THE CROOKHAM GOLF LINKS.

THE Crookham Golf Links are on the fine salubrious common of the same name, and run nearly parallel to the public road leading from Aldermaston to Newbury, which the course crosses once in going out and once in coming in; they are distant about four and a half miles from Newbury, and about a mile from the Thatcham Station of the Great Western Railway, on the branch from Reading to Hungerford.

There is a small club room at the Traveller's Friend, situated a couple of hundred yards from the first tee. In the accompanying rough sketch the greens are marked *, and the arrow heads at the ends of the lines indicate the line of approach. The distances *direct* between the holes amount together to three miles—100yds., the approach course being three miles + 85yds.; they are eighteen in number, and two of them are used both in going out and coming in.

No. 1 is approached by the open ground to the right, lying between the road and the whins. Two good drives will take you to a good lie (avoiding some ruts) on the edge of a shallow gravel pit, whence a good iron shot will land you on the green platform at the further end of it, and close to the hole.

No. 2 is also approached to the right of the direct line, and more or less so as you may play to carry the whins by a long drive, or drive through an opening more to the right on to the straight course; two more drives and a cleek shot will take you home.

No. 3 takes two drives and a short iron shot or long put; is approached by carrying a patch of heather about 120yds. off, or by playing through the open ground to the right of it.

No. 4. Carry a similar patch of heather about 120yds. in front, avoiding two deep narrow ditches, and a second drive will take you within putting distance.

No. 5. An avenue of highish trees crosses the course obliquely at about 120yds., and can be carried by a good drive; this lands you in some rather mossy grass, whence a long spoon and a grass club will take you to the green, keeping clear of a point of whin and heather lying to the right.

No. 6. A small whin lies in front of the tee, and a patch of mixed whin and heather lies in the way of the second drive; but you can play either to the right or left of it, the left being the safest, and a good cleek shot will take you up. The course has lately been rather narrow; but

Nos. 7 and 8 out, and 9 and 10 in, are all plain sailing, with plenty of room, reminding one of the old "Elysian Fields" of Westward Ho.

No. 11. The approach is interfered with by a patch of whin and heather, which takes a long drive to carry; but there is room on either side, and a second good drive will take you within an iron shot of the hole, which requires careful play, as there are several hazards round it.

No. 12 cannot be played direct, as a point of whin and heather, too far to carry, projects on the left. Keeping clear of this, two good drives and a cleek shot will take you home.

No. 13 can be played direct, by carrying the end of an avenue of trees, by a lofting long spoon stroke, and laying your ball on the green in one.

No. 14, also a short hole over the open, is easily reached in one shot. This is the same hole as No. 4 going out.

No. 15. Play to the right of a patch of heather—two drives and a cleek shot.

No. 16. Play direct, carrying a patch of heather, but short of some bad ruts; then a good cleek shot home. Same hole as No. 2 going out.

No. 17. Two good drives to the left of the road, which you have then to cross, avoiding a trappy little ditch on each side of it, by an iron shot to the green close beyond it.

No. 18. Play direct to the right of the road, but carefully for a lie, as there are several little rushy dips in the way. Two drives and a cleek shot to the green, which completes the round.

The distances are as follows:

	Yds. direct.			Yds. direct.
1. Pit Hole	380	10. Whin Hole		250
2. Rut ,,	285	11. Straits ,,		310
3. Sidepath (out)	960	12. Lodge ,,		315
4. Lawn (out)	220	13. Avenue ,,		150
5. Dardanelles	370	14. Lawn (in)		140
6. Pond ,,	335	15. Sidepath (in)		270
7. Road ,,	570	16. Rut (in)		210
8. Turn ,,	285	17. Trap ,,		310
9. Gate ,,	350	18. End ,,		380

The game is played according to the Crookham Club rules, which are copied from those at St. Andrews, with a few trifling exceptions rendered necessary by local circumstances.

Any further information will be readily supplied on application to the hon. sec. of the club, Capt. R. Dashwood Fowler, R.N., Speen Hill, near Newbury.

The Field July 26th 1873

Following the advice of Col. Kennard and other experienced golfers, the committee have somewhat altered the course, and placed some holes in places which present much greater difficulties than formerly.

The neighbourhood of Crookham possesses unusual advantages to golfers; in addition to the fine healthy air on the common, with the splendid views of Hampshire, there are many good residences near; three packs of hounds, the Craven, Vine and South Berks, are within easy access, and there is good shooting and fishing. The number of members of the Golf Club is steadily increasing, and it is fully expected that the attendance of players will be more numerous when the weather becomes cooler.

In our notice of "Golf in Berkshire" in *The Field* of July 5, it was stated that "to the honorary secretary, Capt. Fowler, R.N., belonged the credit of initiating golf at Crookham. We are informed, however, that the Rev. J. Scott Ramsay had been playing golf on the common for some months before anyone else took it up, having procured a set of clubs from St Andrews and commenced play over the ground in May last year, some time before he knew that a brother golfer could be found in the neighbourhood.

In the autumn Capt. Dashwood Fowler, on his return from Westward Ho! – where the idea of the suitability of Crookham Heath for the game occurred to him – entered heartily into the project, and assisted materially in the formation of the Crookham club. It is due to Mr. Ramsay to make the above statement. We are also informed that, in the absence of the hon. sec., any communications on the subject of golf, addressed to "The Committee, Traveller's Friend, Crookham, Newbury" will receive immediate attention.

The Field February 28th 1874

Although no reports have recently appeared of the proceedings of this club, it must not be inferred that the members have been idle. Hunting and shooting have to a certain extent interfered with the play generally, but zeal and keenness for the game have been exhibited on the part of a "band of brothers" whom neither wind, rain, nor even fog have deterred from a journey by rail and putting in an appearance on both club days but notably on Fridays. The Rev. Messrs Jenkinson and Scott Ramsay, Messrs. Mercer, P. Finch, C. Stephens, Thackwell, Berkeley Monck, the secretary, Capt. Dashwood Fowler, &c., have been constant in their attendance. The last named has unfortunately been hors de combat, and will still be so for some little time, in consequence of a heavy fall when hunting with the South Berks, resulting in a fracture of the right arm close to the shoulder. It is hoped, however, that in another month or six weeks he will again be able to wield his clubs. We are authorised to state that the secretary presents a silver challenge cup, of appropriate design, to be competed for by members of any recognised and established golf club on the Crookham links; to be challenged twice in the year, in the spring and autumn, and to become the property of any gentleman who shall play for and win it for the fourth time. It is also hoped that a "champion" prize, confined to members of the club, and to be challenged once a month, may soon be established. It is further to be observed, that one hazard less exists on the links, as that "third party", the ambitious pig, has become bacon!

The Field July 25th 1874

At the general meeting of the Crookham Golf Club, held on the 17th inst., it was resolved that a professional be at once secured to keep the ground in order, and to be ready at a reasonable charge to play with anyone who came over. It was felt to be essential to the well being of a golf club that the links should be kept in good order, and that beginners should have the option of professional instruction when they desired it. It is a great convenience, too, to be able to get clubs and balls on the spot, and to have repairs executed promptly. To meet the increased expenditure, it was resolved that the subscription of playing members, living within thirty miles of Crookham, should be a guinea per annum, the subscription of playing members living beyond that distance, officers from Aldershot, and honorary members being as before, half a guinea. It was decided that all the office-bearers of the club should be elected annually. Those for the present year are Capt. D. Fowler, hon sec. and treasurer; the committee consists of Messrs. Ramsay, Jenkinson, Lyon, Capt. Hodgson, R.N., G. Bulkley, and Stephens.

The Field August 15th 1874

The professional is to make his appearance on the 19th, in time for the competition for the Handicap Cup, now in the possession of Mr. Berkeley Monck, which takes place on Friday the 21st. As the weather is more favourable now for golfing, it is hoped that there will be a good muster of members and their friends on Friday next, and, from the fact of odds being liberally allowed, each one has a fair chance of success. The shooting season has not commenced, and the links are looking their best, so a capital opportunity is presented to sportsmen of getting in condition for the 1st. There is always a breeze, occasionally a gale of wind, and the views of the Hampshire Hills are very fine from all parts of the common. We repeat that the Handicap Challenge Cup is to be played for on Friday next, the 21st August.

The Field August 29th 1874

The professional has come! The satisfaction afforded to the members of the Crookham Golf Club by the advent of T. Manzie from St Andrews, is so great that they desire to record it by the above brief but most interesting announcement. Golfing under difficulties will not now be the rule, we trust, but the exception. We would not desire (unless on cup days, when we are painfully reminded of their existence) the removal of the natural difficulties of the links in the shape of gorse and heather; but we do desiderate greatly the doing away with minor impediments on the putting greens. Manzie, the professional, it is hoped, will soon effect a decided improvement in the ground near the holes.

Manzie made this club after his move to Blackheath in 1876

Golf courses in Scotland in those days had many teaching professionals attached to them, and Manzie was probably one of these.

He appears in reports of St Andrews matches prior to 1875, playing alongside many renowned golfers of the day, including Old Tom Morris.

A month after his arrival, Manzie played a challenge match against Bob Kirk, the Blackheath professional, and won impressively by 2 and 1.

Unfortunately Crookham could not sustain the luxury of a professional and Manzie was released.

In June 1876 he moved to Blackheath, by coincidence replacing Bob Kirk, who returned to Scotland. At Blackheath Manzie received £1 per week throughout the whole term of his employment, supplemented by a payment of 10 shillings every two or three weeks for cleaning the billiard table, and 5 shillings extra on medal days.

His last payment at Blackheath was March 1885 after which he has not been traced.

The Field June 3rd 1876

> Since Manzie's departure for Blackheath the ground has been placed under the care of Harry Baker, a boy of only fifteen years of age, and all agreed he deserved great credit for the order in which the greens were prepared and thanks to Mr. Hutchinson – who though not a golfer himself, is always ready to help the club, and supplied roller, horse and man – the course was never in better order.

The Founders

Midshipman R. Dashwood Fowler

Robert Dashwood Fowler was born in 1814, the son of Rear Admiral R.M. Fowler. His mother died when he was two years old. Her maiden name was Dashwood, and this is perpetuated as a christian name in the ensuing family history.

Fowler entered the Royal Naval College in 1826 and from 1828 served at sea off the coasts of Africa and North America, the Caribbean and the Mediterranean. He spent four years serving on the Canton River, ending his career on the flagship at Portsmouth.

Fowler was a skilled artist and his family possess a collection of drawings and watercolours which beautifully illustrate his career, particularly the years spent in China.

Captain Fowler R.N., retired from the navy in 1846 and died in 1895. Having spent most of his years at sea, it is unlikely that he played golf before his retirement, but by 1872 he was playing at Westward Ho! in foursomes matches, and in 1873, playing in the Sir J. Hope Grant Challenge Medal, won by George Gossett with 101, Captain Fowler was last with 141. In the same week, playing in the Silver Medal and Montcrief Cross, won by J.C. Baldwin with 101, Captain Fowler was last with 158.

The trip to Westward Ho! was a long one and Fowler must have been relieved to learn that not only was there another golfer in the Newbury area, the Rev. John Scott Ramsay, but that he was actually striking golf balls on nearby Crookham Common.

Together, with advice and encouragement from players at Westward Ho!, they planned their golf course. Crookham Common was ideal in many ways. The texture of the heath, with its natural gorse and heather was very suitable, and The Traveller's Friend, as a headquarters, and Thatcham Station to receive its visitors, were other vitally important factors.

The Traveller's Friend was built in the same year, but which came first? It is unlikely that a golf course would have been started where it was, without a headquarters. More probably the plot was hatched in the new inn, with encouragement from the landlord.

Fowler was then living at Speen Hill, Newbury. He made his last appearance at Crookham in September 1875, before moving to London. He never returned, as did the Rev. J. Scott Ramsay, for the regular meetings, nor does he appear in reports in *The Field*, where all competitions and competitors were then recorded.

Apart from being the founder of the club, Fowler was its first secretary and donor of the Open Cup.

Fowler had one daughter, who married Mr J.W. Moir, and they produced nine children, one of whom, Vice Admiral Dashwood F. Moir is mentioned, as is his wife, in reports of golf at Crookham in the 1930s, as winner, in 1936, of the Crookham Challenge Cup (now the Newbury & Crookham Bogey). A son of Vice Admiral Moir, Mr Ian Dashwood Moir, now lives at Beaconsfield. He is a former captain of Newbury Rugby Club and still frequently visits Newbury to watch rugby.

The Reverend John Scott Ramsay was born in Preston in 1843, and a student of St Andrews University from 1859 to 1863, graduating as an MA.

Although described as a "well known player from St Andrews", there is no record of him being a member there, and it seems likely that he was well known simply because he had played at St Andrews. Those learning their golf in the south of England would treat with awe and respect any one known to have set foot on the fairways of St Andrews. He brought his clubs to the Crookham area and played a lonely, improvised, game of golf on the common in 1872.

The first record of his handicap is that he played at Westward Ho! in 1887 off 9. In 1892, his last known visit to Crookham, he was off 16.

At St Andrews University, in addition to classes necessary for gaining his degree of MA, Ramsay also won honours in greek, latin and mathematics. He also studied philosophy, anatomy and physiology. There are nine missing years before he joined his first church at Kingsclere Woodland in Hampshire from 1872 to 1874 (now Ashford Hill church.)

From 1874-1883 he was at Oakley, Hants, but his clerical records show a gap between 1883 and 1900 when he moved to the church of Casterton w Pickworth, living in the rectory at Stamford, Lincolnshire, where he remained until 1921.

After retiring from the church, Ramsay, for 78 years a bachelor, married "the richest woman in Stamford", and moved into her home, Lady Anne's House, where they tutored students hoping to go to Sandhurst.

This venture was short lived, as his wife, sister of the great Olympian, Lord Burghley (Marquis of Exeter), died in 1922.

Ramsay moved to Hoylake, where he became a playing member of Royal Liverpool Golf Club. His membership is recorded there until his death in 1928.

The Reverend John Scott Ramsay at Great Castleton

The first president of Crookham was Albert Richard Tull, born in 1865 and educated at Exeter College, Oxford. He inherited the Crookham estate, and became lord of the manor in 1868. He held the rank of captain in the Royal Berks Yeomanry Cavalry.

He had four daughters and a son. This son, Albert Sancton Blythe, succeeded him as president of Crookham Golf Club. (Blythe being the maiden name of his mother). The youngest daughter Evelyn Mary Bramwell-Davis became president of Crookham ladies golf section.

Tull was high sheriff of Berkshire in 1875, and was chairman of the Newbury Board of Guardians, for 29 years. He played an important role in the administration of the poor law. He was president from 1873 to 1880 and also from 1898 to 1911. He died in 1914.

Albert Richard Tull

By kind permission of Berkshire County Council

The family home was Crookham House, more recently known as Crookham Court School.

Newbury Weekly News May 6th 1875

Crookham Golf Club – The spring meeting of this club will be held on Crookham Common on the 12th, 13th and 14th inst., and on the 11th it is expected that there will be a good number of competitors for the challenge cup, presented by the hon. secretary, Capt. Fowler and open to the members of all established golf clubs; so on that day it is expected the common will be bright with red jackets. As the reason for scarlet having been adopted as the uniform of all golf clubs may not be generally known, we may inform the uninitiated that in ancient times, when the game was first established, a player was not held responsible for any accident or injury caused by his ball, if at the time of striking it he had on a scarlet coat! The attractive colour being intended as a warning to any casual passers-by (while the balls were sent spinning from a distance of perhaps 200 yards) to keep their eyes open! The professional player in charge of the links has now got the course and the putting greens into capital order; and if favoured with fine weather, the votaries of this splendid game are anticipating keen and exciting contests.

Newbury Weekly News September 2nd 1875

The fascination of this fine game has extended to others besides the members of the Crookham Club. For some time past practice has been going on on the Crookham Links, and small subscriptions having accumulated it was arranged to contend for prizes on Saturday the 28th. The day was not very propitious as to weather, but some good play (remarkably so considering the short experience of the players and the limited number of clubs they could afford to provide themselves with) was exhibited. The prizes were awarded as under.

For the best score :
1st   A handsome electro-plate jug – Mr Butler
2nd   A handsome glass and electro-plate butter dish – Mr Holes
3rd   A mustard pot – Mr Nash
4th   A golf club (presented by Mr Manzie, professional to the Crookham Club) – Mr Cheeseman

Extra prize for the best score out, given by Capt. Fowler – six new golf balls – Mr Holes.

With all those who are concerned in the promotion of health-giving athletic sports and in providing counter attractions to those of the beer shop, these proceedings will have an interest; and it is a pity that this game is not more generally known and enjoyed. Without disparaging cricket, golf possesses many advantages over it. It can be played all through the year (except on snow), it does not require the gathering together of 22 players, as any number can take part in it; one can play it even alone, the play is continuous, and not broken by "innings" and "outings"; it tries the temper and the judgement, for it is played with the head as well as the hands; the most accurate precision is attainable, but mediocrity confers also great pleasure after having mastered the rudiments.

One difficulty lies in the way of those who are not rich – the expense of clubs and balls; but this might be met by the formation of a club, with a small subscription, and the proceeds devoted to the provision of tools for the general use of the members. The promotion of this game is commended to the consideration of those who have the welfare of the middle and lower classes at heart.

The Open Challenge Cup

Following the successful launching of the club, the next important events were the arrival of the two silver cups in 1874. These cups are to reappear throughout this book being the most tangible link with our past history.

Captain Dashwood Fowler donated the Open Cup, later known as The Crookham Challenge Cup, and now as the Newbury & Crookham Medal.

The Open Cup was a scratch tournament and, as is evident from the list of winners, drew the best players in the country to Crookham.

The following extract from *The Field* magazine of May 25th 1878, explains its conditions.

The Open Challenge Cup was originally presented to the club by Capt. Fowler R.N. with a condition that it should become the property of anyone who could win it four times. It has now been won twice by three gentlemen, and on the offer being made by Mr E. Gibson to replace it with another if it should be won a third time, it was resolved by acclamation that, subject to the approval of the donor, Mr Gibson's offer be accepted.

Horace Hutchinson was the most prominent golfer of his time. He was born in 1859, and at the age of five his family moved to Northam, (before it became known as Westward Ho!).

The Royal North Devon Golf Club was founded that year, 1864, and his life from that time onwards was devoted to golf.

By the year of the first, unofficial, Open Amateur Championship in 1885, in which he was runner up, he was already a renowned figure both as a golfer and as a writer.

He won the Amateur Championship in 1886 and 1887, and was runner up in 1903.

Books by Hutchinson are in great demand today, his best known probably being the Badminton Library – *Golf* (1890).

In 1911, aged 52, Hutchinson became so seriously ill that he could neither play golf again, nor watch others. He committed suicide in 1932.

The following anecdote appears in Hutchinson's book *Fifty Years of Golf* (1914).

At that time of day (1878) all who were golfers reared on the seaside links had a very high and mighty contempt for all in the shape of inland golf. In spite of the antiquity of Blackheath, the art and labour by which an inland course can be brought up, when the weather is favourable, to a condition almost rivalling that of the seaside links were quite unknown. One of the earliest founded of the inland type – of course long ages after such an ancient institution as Blackheath – was the course at Crookham, near Newbury; and thereby hangs a tale of tragedy and comedy commingled, associated with my golfing days at Oxford. There was a certain trophy, open to all amateur golfers, given by the Club, and called the Crookham Cup. The conditions were that it was to remain as a challenge prize to be played for annually unless and until any man should win it thrice: in which case it should become his property. Poor Herbert Burn, who met his death not so very long after in a steeplechase, had won this cup twice, and I was invited to go to Crookham to see if I could put a check on his victory and keep the cup for the Club. We were hospitably put up for the meeting by Mr Stephens, the banker, at his place near Reading. I had the luck to win the cup, and again, going down the next year, won it again. If I should win it a third time it became my very own, and, strong in the zeal of pot-hunting, I went down the third year too. I remember that on this occasion, for some reason, Mr Stephens did not act host for the meeting, but Captain Ashton and I stayed with Major Charley Welman at a little house he had near the course: and what fixed the visit very firmly in my mind is that Ashton and I returned to the house, after a round on the first day of our arrival, with "dubbed", not blacked, golfing boots. It appeared that there was no "dubbing" in the house, for the next morning our boots were sent up to us black-leaded – with the stuff that grates, I think, are done with. The effect was splendid. We went forth quite argentine as to our understandings, like knights in armour clad, and, thus glistening, I contrived to win that cup for the third and final time, which made it my own. Now we come to the tragi-comedy of the story. On the way back to Oxford there was the inevitable change and wait at Didcot Junction, and there whom should I see, with golf clubs under arm, but George Gossett? He was then living at Abingdon. I greeted him and asked with interest where he was going.

"Well" said he, "there's a cup to be played for at Crookham, near Newbury, to-morrow. I've won it twice and I'm going down to see if I can win it again, because if I do I keep it."

"Oh dear," I had to reply, "I'm sorry, but I'm afraid you must have made a mistake in the day. It's to-day it was played for, and what's more I'd won it twice before, too, and I won it again to-day, so that it's mine now, I'm afraid," and I opened its case, which I had in my hand, and showed it to him. I was obliged to tell him; for it would have been worse still if he'd gone on all the way to Crookham to find he was a day behind the fair. As it was, it was comedy for me, but rather cruel tragedy for him. No man ever took a knock more pleasantly: he was the first to start a laugh against himself and to give me congratulations, and express gratitude for being saved the journey to Crookham. So he took train to Abingdon and I to Oxford, and shortly after, whether as the effect or no of his blow, he went out to New Zealand, where he won the championship of that country more than once.

What used to astonish all my friends in College almost more than anything else, when I used vainly to try to describe to them what manner of game golf is, was the fact that I did not "dress" for it. "Undress" is rather what they meant. You see, they were accustomed to cricket, where you flannelled yourself, and to football, rowing and athletic sports wherein the mode of dress was to have as little of it as might decently be, and that one should go forth in the very clothes in which you might attend a lecture and play a game in them seemed hardly thinkable. They used to take up the clubs and regard them curiously. They began to think there must be something more than they had supposed in the game when I showed them the Crookham Cup.

Open Challenge Cup Winners

1874	Spring	G. Gossett (Royal North Devon)	94
	Autumn	G. Gossett (Royal North Devon)	94
1875	Spring	Capt. Cecil Lyon (Crookham)	92
	Autumn	Rev. J. Scott Ramsay (Crookham)	
1876	Spring	Steven Smith (Blackheath)	95
	Autumn	R.W.S. Vidal (Crookham)	95
1877	Spring	H.W. Burn (Royal North Devon)	
	Autumn	H.W. Burn (Royal North Devon)	
1878	Spring	H. Hutchinson (Royal North Devon)	93
	Autumn	H. Hutchinson (Royal North Devon	84
1879	Spring	H. Hutchinson (Royal North Devon)	

(George Gossett became a member in 1876 when he moved into the county).

According to the revised terms attached to the cup, Hutchinson became its new owner, but unfortunately this was the last meeting of its kind, and the offer of a replacement cup by Mr E. Gibson was never taken up. The story of the Open Cup and of its return to Crookham is continued later.

In the book quoted, Hutchinson refers to the Oxford Cambridge matches, when he again remembers Crookham:

> There was in existence that course at Crookham, near Newbury, which would have been convenient to us from Oxford; but it would not at all so well have suited the Cambridge men. Besides there was little play on it except at the meeting times, and the course was not permanently kept in any order. It is worth mentioning that for one of the holes, a short hole, the play was over an avenue of tall trees. In the years since, while inland courses have been multiplying, so too have the tree hazards at the sides. Here we have them in a line right across the course, and you have to be over. It was not a "blind" hole, for you could just get a glimpse of the flag between the stems. Some of our course constructors might make a note of this hole; and might do worse than copy it. At the same time, I should say that one of its kind in a round is enough.

The hole referred to in this piece was the 13th (The Avenue), but Hutchinson had obviously forgotten, when writing the last sentence, that the same trees were in play across the 5th (Dardanelles). The avenue of lime trees, still visible today, is the only remaining landmark of the old course.

Although Hutchinson shows some appreciation of Crookham in his reminiscences, he, and his contemporaries, generally believed that the only real golf was "links" golf.

The Crookham Handicap Challenge Cup

Known today as the Newbury & Crookham Bogey, this cup was presented to the club by Mr Charles Stephens of Woodley Hill, Earley, Reading, in 1874. The first winner was C. S. Cunliffe (92nd Regt., Aldershot), but there were many more in the next six years, as the cup was played for as often as twice in a month.

The holder was challenged by the winner of a qualifying round. Sometimes only two would attempt to qualify. Should only one show willing, he would directly challenge the holder. If the holder failed to appear to defend his cup, the challenger would win it by default.

When, in 1993, the honours boards in the clubhouse were being renewed, the names of the early holders of the cup were consigned to history.

The Club Cup was played for monthly by members, off handicap. It did not reappear when the club was re-opened in 1891.

HANDICAP CUP			CLUB CUP	
(Newbury & Crookham Bogey)			(No longer in existence)	

		HANDICAP CUP	CLUB CUP
1874	May 1st	C.S. Cunliffe (92nd Regt. Aldershot)	
	May 4th	Capt. Cecil Lyon	
	June 5th	Rev J. Scott Ramsay	
	June 19th	Rev J. Scott Ramsay	
	July 17th	Rev J. Scott Ramsay	
	July 25th	Berkeley Monck	
	August	J. Garland	
	September	Rev. J. Scott Ramsay (w-o)	Rev. J. Scott Ramsay
	September	Mr Morley	
	October	Capt. Cecil Lyon	
	November	Capt. Cecil Lyon	
	December	Capt. Cecil Lyon	Rev J. Scott Ramsay
1875	January	H.C. Rogers	
	February	Capt. R. Dashwood Fowler	Rev. J. Scott Ramsay
	March	Capt. Cecil Lyon	
	April	Capt. Cecil Lyon	
	May	Capt. Cecil Lyon	Capt. Cecil Lyon
	May	Capt. R. Dashwood Fowler	Capt. Cecil Lyon
	June	C. Stephens	Capt. R. D. Fowler
	July	C. Stephens	Capt. R. D. Fowler
	August	Rev. J. Scott Ramsay	
	September	J.H. Morley	Rev. J. Scott Ramsay
	November	Rev. E.D. Prothero	
	December	C. Stephens	Rev. E.D. Prothero
1876	May	Rev. J. Scott Ramsay	Rev. J. Scott Ramsay
	June	Rev. J. Scott Ramsay	Rev. J. Scott Ramsay
	November	J.C. Maclaren	R.W.S. Vidal
	December	Col. Briggs	Col. Briggs
1877	January	Capt. A. Markham	Rev. H.C. Rogers
	February	C. Stephens	C. Stephens
1878	May	Rev. T. Goddard	J.C. Maclaren
	August	J.C. Maclaren	J.C. Maclaren
	November	H. Hutchinson (Royal North Devon)	H. Hutchinson (Royal North Devon)
1880	April	A.H. Molesworth (Royal North Devon)	A.H. Molesworth (Royal North Devon)

When the club closed, in 1880, the Handicap Cup was handed over to Westward Ho!, where it was played for as the Crookham Handicap Cup. Its winners, recorded below, include five presidents of Royal North Devon. Also on the list are the now familiar names of Gossett, Horace Hutchinson and, in 1887, "our own" J. Scott Ramsay.

1881	H. Hutchinson	82-Scr-82	(President 1886)
1882	B. James	112-27-85	
1883	C.R. Smith	115-28-87	
1884	F. Gossett	89-9-80	
1885	W.F. Ashton	91-4-87	(President 1885)
1886	B. Nixon		
1887	J.S. Ramsay	91-9-82	
1888	J.C. McClaren	90-1-89	(President 1890)
1889	A.L. Christie	104-18-86	
1890	C.A. Pidock	102-17-85	
1891	A.L. Christie	98-13-85	(President 1903)
1892	P. Winterscale	102-27-85	(President 1895)
1893	C.A. Pidock	98-13-85	

In Autumn 1893 the cup was returned to Crookham.

Francis Powell Hopkins (1830-1913) was a journalist for *The Field* magazine from the late 1860s, writing under the name of "Shortspoon". Today he is renowned for his paintings, which provide a valuable contribution to the history of golf. He illustrated personalities and courses of his day, in particular Royal North Devon, where he was a member.

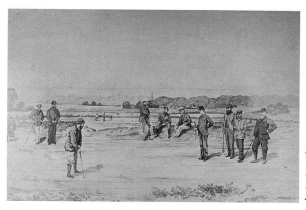

Early golf at Crookham from a watercolour by Major F.P.Hopkins

The following extract is from *The Field*, August 1878, in reference to the Crookham autumn meeting.

> Some of the party indulged in foursomes in the afternoon, while the Major, with the assistance of a very small boy and a very large umbrella, took some rapid sketches of some of the prominent features of the links which will shortly be added to his well-known series of golfing sketches.

A completed painting was presented to Horace Hutchinson at the spring meeting in 1879.

The development of golf at Crookham was a convenient link between the other three golfing venues in the south of England, Westward Ho!, Blackheath and Wimbledon.

Crookham could claim to be only the third 18 hole course in England, the others being at Westward Ho! and Hoylake, and it was certainly the first 18 hole "inland" course. It was therefore a great attraction, and the best golfers in England were keen to travel many miles to compete in the popular spring and autumn meetings.

Club memberships then were mostly made up of landowners, masons, bankers, flourishing tradesmen, and, well represented, the church.

There was growth and success in the early years, and an evident sense of pioneering, but growth was an enemy to Crookham, and through lack of support, the club folded in 1880.

The Field April 17th 1880

> Although this little club, owing to the migration of nearly all the local players, has almost ceased to exist, and there has been no play since June last, a few of the old 'habitue' came down for an Easter holiday and played in most glorious weather.
>
> The ground was got into some little order at short notice, but was very rough. On Monday thirteen players competed for the club and handicap cups in one round.

This was the last golf played at Crookham until 1891.

Crookham Members 1873 – 1880

1873	A.R. Tull (president, non golfer)	1875	H.C. Rogers
	Captain Dashwood Fowler		Rev. V.G. Faithful
	Rev. J. Scott Ramsay		Dr. W.L. Purves
	Mr Thackwell (Thatcham)		(Royal & Ancient, Blackheath)
	G. Bulkley		W.F. Lyon
	E. Scratton		M. Rogers
	Rev. J.H. Jenkinson		Rev. E.D. Prothero
	P. Finch		(Turweston, Bucks)
	C. Stephens (Reading)		E.W. Hawker
	Berkeley Monck		Rev. H.W. Hussey "an
	R.S. Cunliffe (93rd Regt. Aldershot)		ethusiastic novice"(St. Pauls,
	Captain Cecil Lyon (Burghfield)		Great Portland Street, London)
	-. Mercer (Westward Ho!)		Stephen Smith
	Rev. T. Goddard (Hungerford)		Col. Kennard (Blackheath)
	E. Gibson	1876	A.W. McDonnell
	Bland Garland and brother		A.T. Scott
1874	Fitzroy Moncrieff		J.C. McClaren
	H. Fowler-Jones		Capt. Johnson
	-. Shuter		Col. Briggs
	Capt. Hodgson		D. Mason
	Rev. G.S.C. Jenkinson		Capt. C. Borrer
	F. Fowler		G. Gossett (Weswsard Ho!)
	G. Fowler	1877	Rev. J. Clemenson
	H. Morley		Rev. W. Lysaght (Sherfield on
	R. W. S. Vidal		Loddon, Basingstoke)
			G. Wylie
			G.F. Muir

Dr W.Laidlaw Purves MD first played at Crookham in 1875. He was an eye specialist, and was a member of the R&A, Royal Blackheath, the Hon. Company of Edingburgh Golfers, Royal Wimbledon (captain 1897-8) and Royal St George's at which he was a pioneer and where the picture shown above now hangs. Purves was also a great supporter of ladies golf, being instrumental in the Ladies Golf Union being formed in 1893.

2

The Second Phase 1891-1914

The Rev. Herbert Henry Skrine, vicar of Greenham Church, formerly curator of St Nicolas Church, Newbury, was honorary secretary and treasurer of Crookham Golf Club from 1891 to 1900. He was presented with a retirement gift at the 1900 AGM, at the Volunteer Inn, and his reply was reported as follows:

> On an occasion of this character one recalled old faces and old scenes, and he was pleased to see his old friend Mr Spurway present, who, in conjunction with Mr A.B. Cooke, and one or two others, was instrumental in re-introducing golf into this locality. In those days (1890) they played on a course prepared by Mr Cooke on Snelsmore Common and subsequently in a hayfield at Donnington where one gallant old golfer played everyday. This was not good enough and they removed to Crookham where he well remembered searching for the holes that were used on the old course, in company with Mr Spurway.

The first mention of golf after 1880 appeared in the *Newbury Weekly News* in June 1891.

William George Mount
President 1891–1897

A correspondent gives some interesting reminiscences of Crookham Golf Club, which has just recently been revived under the active and judicious management of the Vicar of Greenham (Rev. H.H. Skrine). When one thinks of the progress golf has made in popular estimation, it is hard to realise that only twenty years ago a solitary golfer (The Rev. J. Scott Ramsay) might have been seen playing on the pleasant common of Crookham in Berkshire, literally astonishing the natives, who could not understand what the white and red flags were meant for, and why such a collection of clubs should be carried. In the course of a few months, some members of the Westward Ho! club (Capt. R. Dashwood Fowler), who lived in the neighbourhood, began to play and ere long a successful club was started.

There can be no question of the beauty of the views from the common and the fine healthy air one breathes there, furthermore it may unhesitatingly be claimed for the Crookham links that it is one of the most sporting inland courses to be found anywhere.

Newbury pre 1900

It is a very trying one for beginners who, when they see a flag marking a hole which they wish to approach, whatever hazards may be in view, promptly seize their drivers and do their best. Certain wary old golfers may be observed using their irons to get near enough to clear the obstacles with their second shots. It cannot be said that such cautious policy is invariably attended with success.

There are already some fifty members and it may be anticipated others will be glad to join.

There were two major changes in the situation at Crookham now. The Traveller's Friend gave way to The Volunteer Inn as headquarters, a considerable event, since The Traveller's Friend was at the farthest point from Newbury, and The Volunteer Inn, at the nearest.

To enable the lst tee to be adjacent to the new headquarters, the order of play was manipulated so that players went away from Newbury, turning at the 11th tee to return. This point lies in front of the old Crookham laundry, which still stands just off the Brimpton Road. The changes meant that the whole course was then on the north, Thatcham side, of the Brimpton Road. The first 500 yards of the old course, which began from 200 yards short of The Traveller's Friend, on the opposite side of the road, were given up.

In 1890 a Mr Marsh was employed to rediscover and reconstruct the golf course, but in the following year Mr A.S. Denness took over. For the next four years Denness won constant praise for his development of the course, especially the greens. During this period, in 1893, the new landlord of The Volunteer Inn, G.W. Millsom arrived. The Volunteer Inn being the headquarters of the club, Millsom became its caterer and during the next 25 years he was variously described as steward, greenkeeper, professional and clubmaker. Millsom left The Volunteer Inn in 1918. There is no evidence that he ever played golf. This was a period of consolidation, and it is evident that strong characters such as Skrine, Evans, Denness, and Millsom enabled the reborn club to gain strength quickly. By 1892, permanent caddies were employed and the membership was up to 87.

The minutes of the AGM, February 4th 1892 read as follows:

> It must be remembered that the club only re-started in May last year and the accounts do not represent twelve months outlay, and consequently it is obvious that the position of the club financially will demand consideration of the members. The prize fund has not yet met with the attention it deserves from many of the members, but it is hoped that ere long the club may be in a position to purchase the new Open Challenge Cup.

By May 1893 the prize fund had reached £8, but it was never used for the purchase of replacements for the two main events, as the two original cups – the Members Challenge Cup and the Open Cup, found their way back to Crookham via Westward Ho!

Anticipating the purchase of new cups the titles were played for from Whitsun 1891, and it was a coincidence that the first winner of the Members Challenge Cup on its return was the Rev. J. Stewart who had himself brought the cup back from Royal North Devon, where it had been played for for the previous 12 years. How did he persuade them to part with it? This was the first time the cup was used for a bogey competition, for which it has been used ever since.

There is no report of how and when the Open Cup found its way back to Crookham. Having been won outright by Horace Hutchinson in 1879, and he being a member of Royal North Devon, it would seem likely that he generously paired his cup with the Members Challenge Cup, so that they could both return to their rightful home.

The second era of Crookham, beginning in 1891, was dominated by many new names. Prominent were those of seven masters from the new Horris Hill School, three miles from Crookham. Albert Henry Evans was founder of the school, which was intended to be a "feeder" school for Winchester College.

Evans was on the Crookham committee from the beginning of this period, being the first ever appointed club captain in 1892, retaining the post in 1893.

Horris Hill school teachers 1901. L.V.Lodge is extreme left, Evans seated centre. Five of the others were members

Born in 1858, Evans gained rugby and cricket blues at Oxford. His record in the varsity matches included 1878 – 12 for 141, 1880 – 10 for 133, 1881 – 13 for 130 (including hat trick, as captain).

He was a fast bowler and in the 1879 varsity match bowled unchanged throughout both innings. Evans appeared in seven Gentlemen v Players matches between 1878-1885, each time playing alongside W.G. Grace, in the last of which he took 7 for 23 off 31 overs!

Evans was twice picked to play rugby for England, but was unable to play on either occasion.

He took up golf in 1891 and by 1894 was a scratch player. Other players from the staff of Horris Hill School were: Bernard Rendall (5), who had played football for Harrow School (Captain 1883) and Cambridge;

J.H. Haviland (5), E.J. Maguire (3), R.A. Ingram (9) and J.L. Stow (12). Maguire, Rendall and Ingram also played football for Newbury.

In October 1891 the mythical Cup was won by B. Rendall, this time in a handicap tournament.

The full scores were:

B Rendall	120-24=96	(5)
R.J. Maguire	117-20=97	(3)
A.H. Evans	116-18=98	(Scr)
J.H. Morley	118-15=103	(10)
Rev. J. Stewart	118-14=104	(8)
Rev. R.P. Spurway	124-18=106	(8)
A.C. Bartholomew	132-18=114	(8)
J.H. Haviland	136-22=114	(5)
H.G. Fane – no return		

The figures on the right show the lowest handicap attained by each of these players within the next four years. Most were either new golfers or starved of golf, and skill was as yet undeveloped. It seems that, to restart the club, handicaps were pitched at a high level, and those with talent were soon able to adjust, assisted by a system which made it possible to leap, mostly downwards, by ten shots in a year!

Completing the group from Horris Hill, in 1895, was Lewis Vaughan Lodge who played football for Cambridge and the Corinthians, and won three international caps for England at full-back ".... a red headed and courageous tackler ....".

Lodge, who was Crookham secretary from 1910 to 1914, died by drowning in 1916.

J.L. Stow bought Horris Hill School from Evans in 1918. His son Jimmy, who also taught there, now retired, provided the following extract from an unpublished book by his father *Life at Horris Hill*, (1902).

> I remember a fortnight after I arrived (Sept '02) all the masters, Evans, Haviland, Maguire, Lodge, Ingram and I went to Crookham to play golf – Autumn medal – leaving Hidden to deal with the school single handed till our return, which he managed without difficulty.

Newbury Weekly News Oct 1891 "May we ask equestrians to kindly ride clear of the putting greens which have been placed, after much consideration, where it is thought that they will be the least interference with the freedom of the general public".

Visit of J.H. Taylor

When J.H. Taylor visited Crookham on November 1st 1893 the event passed without comment in the local newspaper, but was mentioned in the AGM report of February 1894:

> J.H. Taylor, the Winchester professional, playing with Mr E.H.R. Buckland[1] and Captain Russell, for the first time on the links, in spite of a very strong wind, and driving rain, made the fine score of 83, namely 43 out and 40 home.

Within a year Taylor had won the first of his five Open Championships, at Sandwich.

At Crookham, Taylor's caddie was a 14 year old named Walter Edwin Clinch, later to become the Crookham professional.

In a report of the autumn meeting in October 1894, it was stated that:

> The club is steadily increasing its membership, the course itself proving more and more its own recommendation as it becomes better known. Thatcham Station, 1.5 miles only from its headquarters, The Volunteer Inn, brings the links within easy reach of Reading, and even the Metropolis itself.

Clinch was born only a short distance from the course. He was to remain with the club until its demise in 1940, with periods of absence for the Boer War, and the First World War.

The minutes of the annual general meeting for 1900 show some notable changes. Rev. H.H. Skrine, who was moving to Maidenhead, resigned as secretary, after nine years, having steered the club since its reopening in 1891. He was replaced by Mr C.H.H. Macartney. In 1905, Macartney gave way to Mr E.M. Fowler who had been acting as assistant secretary.

The following description of the course appeared in *A History of Berkshire* (part 16) in 1906:

> The oldest golf club in Berkshire is the Crookham Golf Club, which has the respectable antiquity of close on thirty years. It was founded in 1873, when a good inland course was laid out on Crookham Common near Newbury. The course of 18 holes, which is nearly three miles in length, is on a high table-land with a gravel soil, where heather and whins flourish to the confusion of the player who does not drive far and sure. The hazards are all natural, and consist of roads, gravel pits, formidable stretches of heath and gorse, and a pond that has spoilt many a promising medal round.

---

[1] E.H.R. Buckland was a teacher at Winchester College. He won a cricket blue at Oxford and was a scratch golfer at Crookham.

Straight driving is essential to success, for the course is narrow and bordered with rough grass and whins. The greens are large, and afford interesting putting, and the lies are almost uniformly good on the short crisp turf of that breezy upland. The par score for the 18 holes is 80. Play is possible all the year round, though the best time for the game is in the winter, spring, and early summer. Accommodation for golfers is to be found at the Volunteer Inn on Crookham Common, where are the club-room and head quarters of the club. Meetings are held in the spring and autumn, when the principal prize for competition is a valuable challenge cup.

Membership was by this time just short of 100, and the officers of the club were well satisfied with its progress, especially with the balance in hand of £25.16s.4d.

Subscriptions were £1 per annum.

Millsom was referred to as greenkeeper at the 1894 AGM, but by October 1895 the club had employed G. Founds as professional and greenkeeper. He was only to stay for two years.

It was at this time, in 1895, that there was first mentioned the prospect of building a new clubhouse, to include ... "a sitting room and a room for ladies, and dressing room, drying room, and caddies shelter".

It is significant that there was consideration for ladies, although they were to be segregated. This was the first mention of women in connection with golf since the birth of the club 22 years earlier.

Apart from those already mentioned, other playing members in 1896 were: R.G. Durrant, J.J. Ridley, R.B. King, A.H. Worrell, G.M Fowler, Rev. G.A. Hicks, Captain A.B. Ridley, R.H. Noot, W.G. Fellows, H.R. Gifford, F.N. Garry, J.T. Jackson, C.F. Osborne, Major Lockhart, Lieut. Lockhart, R. Brooks King, P.T. Baker. Also of note are the names of well known local businessmen, G.T. Metcalf, W.H. Belcher and G.S. Edwards.

At the annual general meeting of February 1896, it was recorded that:

The professional, G. Founds, has proved himself useful to many of the members, both in coaching and playing, his best round being 37 out, 39 back, total 76.

On the same occasion in 1897:

The club has, after much consideration, decided to dispense with the services of the professional G. Founds, since the amount of play on the links does not justify the outlay in this respect, and it would be better for him to seek an engagement elsewhere. He plays a good game and is a quite respectable young man, and hails from Westward Ho!

Through the exertion of Mr F.N. Garry, an arrangement has been entered into with the Great Western Railway Company whereby members can travel to and fro the links at a considerable reduction in fares.

Officers on the active list stationed in the neighbourhood are admitted under favourable terms.

Strangers can now play rounds on the links at a cost of 1/- a day or 2/6 a week, provided that they are members of a recognised golf club.

As there were no other golf clubs within easy reach of Crookham, the above report seems scarcely to encourage local people to take up the game.

In the spring of 1897 W.E. Clinch was appointed as club professional, replacing G. Founds. He fitted in quite quickly both as greenkeeper and professional, immediately setting a professional record of 74. H.E. Meek had set a course record of 74 the previous year.

The period from 1906 until the First World War was one of routine club life, with no further pioneering to be done, nor fears for the future.

The spring and autumn meetings continued to be the high points of each year.

Surprisingly throughout this period no other trophies were added to the existing bogey and medal cups, and these, having been played for twice a year until 1900, were, from then, played for only annually. However, at regular, and other meetings there were prizes to be competed for, usually donated by officers of the club.

F. Dodd, was first mentioned as "keeper of the golf links" in 1906. As W. Dodd he was called "greenkeeper" in 1906; again as F. Dodd, he was entitled "professional" in the *Golfers Handbook* of 1911, and in a newspaper report in 1912 he was referred to as "greenkeeper". By 1914 he was restored to "golf links keeper".

The post of honorary secretary again changed hands. In 1908 Mr Broome Pinnegar took over from E. Fowler, who retained the post of honorary treasurer. In 1910 L.V. Lodge of Horris Hill School became secretary and remained so until golf ceased in 1914. The secretary's report in 1910 included the following plea:

> May I in conclusion appeal to those who ride down the course to keep as far from the putting greens as possible, and if in wet weather they would refrain from cantering down the course, they would earn the respect of every golfer for their kindly consideration of another's pleasure.

In 1911, for the first time in the 38 years since its conception, Crookham recorded the names of ladies in a match report reproduced in the *Newbury Weekly News*: Crookham Ladies lost 4-1 to Winchester Ladies, their only winner being Miss M. Stokes. Others in the team were Miss S. Stokes, Miss S. Kitcat, Mrs P. Bramwell Davis and Miss Ivy Arbuthnot.

Newbury Weekly News 1912

The second annual supper given to the commoners by the members of Crookham Golf Club was held at the Volunteer Inn on Friday last. There were about forty present and after ample justice had been done to the excellent fare provided by Mr & Mrs Millsom and Mr Fry, the rest of the evening was spent in speeches and music. The chair was taken by Mr L.V. Lodge who, after the Kings' health, proposed the health of the commoners. Excellent songs were given by Messrs Cook, Tidbury, Anderson, Buckle, Millsom and others, and a most enjoyable evening was brought to a close by the singing of 'Auld Lang Syne' and 'God Save the King' at ten o'clock.

Willie, Tony and Lottie Dod

In 1905 Charlotte (Lottie) Dod, and her two older brothers Willie and Tony sold their family home in the Wirral, and moved to Newbury. It was the family tradition to name their houses "Edge ...." to honour the memory of Sir Anthony Dod of Edge, who had commanded the English archers at Agincourt, from whom the family claimed descent. They named their house in Andover Road, Edgecombe.

Lottie Dod was the greatest sportswoman of her time, perhaps of all time. In each of her five visits to Wimbledon between 1887 and 1893 she was champion, losing only one set. She remains the youngest Wimbledon champion, at fifteen years ten months. She also represented England.

She was a hockey international in 1899, and shot for the United Kingdom archery team in the 1908 Olympic Games, winning a silver medal. Her brother Willie won the men's gold medal.

Lottie started golf at 15, but it was only after retiring from hockey and tennis that she won the British Amateur Ladies Championship at Troon. The following year, she represented England.

Willie and Tony became members of Crookham, Willie serving on the committee, and winning the Crookham Challenge Cup (Newbury & Crookham Medal) in 1911. Lottie did not play in club golf, but would certainly have played with her brothers at Crookham.

They left Newbury in 1912.

Willie died in 1954. Tony died in 1960 and six months later Lottie died in her 89th year, whilst in bed listening to a radio broadcast from Wimbledon.

Crookham Challenge Cup

(formerly the Open Cup, now the Newbury & Crookham Medal)

1891	October	Rev. B.P. Spurway	115-20-95
1892	May	A.C. Bartholomew	97-18-79
	October	J.C. Bowring	92- 8-84
1893	May	R.S. Wilson	94-14-80

There had been no cup to play for until now, when the original Open Cup, won outright by Horace Hutchinson in 1879, was returned to the club. It was played for as a members scratch championship until 1916.

1893	November	A.H. Evans	92 (whilst club captain)
1894	May	H.E. Meek	84
	October	A.H. Evans	90
1895	May	A.H. Evans	86 (after play off with A.B.Cooke)
	October	A.B. Cooke	86
1896	May	A.B. Cooke	81
	October	A.H. Evans	88
1897	May	W.R. Ridley	86
	October	H.E. Meek	83
1898	May	H.E. Meek	80
	October	J.R. Haviland	90
1899	May	H.E. Meek	85
	October	B. Rendall	88
1900	May	A.H. Evans	85
	October	Torrential rain and strong winds left no survivors	
1901	May	E.M. Fowler	86
	October	E.J. Maguire	86
1902	May	S.S. Wollaston	93
	October	S.S. Wollaston	93
1903		A.H. Evans	
1904		L.V. Lodge	82
1905		J.H. Haviland	86
1906		E.J. Maguire	82
1907		Dr F.P. Joscelyne	83
1908		O.S. Horn	89
1909		O.S. Horn	87
1910		H.D. Wells	88
1911		W. Dod	77
1912		M.O. Wells	85
1913		L.V. Lodge	80
1914		M.O. Wells & H.D. Floyd shared	

The following list shows the year in which members were first mentioned other than those previously featured. These details were only available from reports of competitions and matches.

1897
J.A. Waller
P.A. Underhill
W. Ridley
A.C. Skinner
Dr Jenner Clarke
W.H. Tottle
C.W. Cailes
General Laughton
L. Bury
R.D. Hoyle
M.L. Liebenrood
R.H. Caird
S.S. Wollaston

1898
S.F. Fisher
J.T. Jackson

1899
Capt. F. Maitland
R. Baukes

1900
Rev. S. Angel Smith
J.S. Woods
G.S. Seon

1901
J. Quinn
R.G. Bramwell Davis
Rev. C.H.T. Wood
F.S. Preston
H.H. Marriot

1905
Rev. G. Dangerfield
W. St. Q. Leng
J. Bowman-Smith
H. Copeland
H.L. Cancellor
C.A. Cancellor
O.S. Horn

1906
V.L. Hil
G.R. Tadman
E.M. Fletcher
S. Shelley
A. Tate
W. Dod
A. Dod
O. Newmarch

1908
W.P.Y. Bainbridge
L. Portman
W. Graham-Lloyd

1909
E. Donner
G.S. Fort
S.G. Lloyd
R.C. Thomson
A.G. Witherby

1910
P. Dollar
A.J. Lawson
S.L. Trevor
A.W. Sutton
C.S. Holberton
F. Stokes

1911
J.F. Macdonald
Rev E.P Grundy

1912
F.R. Gosling
L.E. Yeomans

1913
Miss Sandbach
Miss E.F. Guillenard
Mrs G Wells
Miss E. Gosling
Mrs B. Pinnegar
Miss Witherby

1914
A.V. Morris
Dr Martin
L. Portman
Major C. Turner
J.A.H.C. Borgnis
P. Lindley
M.H.F. Sutton
R. Orme
G.S. Barnes
Col. Lyon
A.R. Peart
C.H. Cooke
W.M. Tadd
Carleton Holmes
C.J. Kenrick

3

Between the Wars 1920 – 1930

Golf made a slow return to Crookham after the 1914-1918 war. It was not contemplated until March 1920, and was only restarted at the end of that year when 16 players took part in a competition.

Newbury Weekly News March 18th 1920

Crookham Golf Club to be Re-started – support needed

In response to a general feeling amongst local golfers, a meeting was held in the Lecture Room of the Guildhall Club on Tuesday evening for the purpose of re-starting the Crookham Golf Club. During the war, the club, like many other similar institutions was allowed to lapse, but with the increased popularity of the game, it had been felt for some time that an effort should be made to revive it. Mr. A.S.B. Tull, the Lord of the Manor of Crookham, is very keen on the project, and presided over the gathering, which numbered several members of the old club, including Messrs. A.G. Witherby, Gifford Wells, Maurice Wells, Broome Pinniger, J. Greenshields, F.H. Floyd, S. Hickman, and a large number of the more recent recruits to golf. The Chairman, in opening the proceedings, spoke of the pressing need which existed for a golf club and course in the locality of Newbury, and then invited discussion. Mr. Gifford Wells led the way, throwing out most valuable suggestions for lines upon which the club should be re-formed, and others who took part were Messrs. Witherby, Greenshields, S. Hickman, H.R. Metcalf, A.P. Davies, Hugh Turner, T. Carr and F. Povey.

CROOKHAM GOLF CLUB

TO BE RE-CONSTITUTED.

It was feared with the establishment of the new club at Greenham that the Crookham Golf Club would drop out of existence. We believe that from a sentimental point of view even the members of the new club would regret this, as the Crookham course is the third oldest in England. The affairs of the old club have been wound up, but an effort is being made to continue the course, and especially to run it as an artizan club. With the increasing popularity of golf, this is a step in the right direction. Mr. Moore, the landlord of "The Volunteer," has consented to provide the necessary accommodation for the Club house, to keep the greens in order, and generally supervise the course, and it is hoped to get a sufficient number of members at a guinea apiece to keep the Club going. Mr. Tom Carr, of Cheap-street, is the honorary secretary pro tem., and will be glad to hear of any members who wish to join.

CROOKHAM GOLF CLUB

SUBSCRIPTIONS are due from MAY 1st:—

GENTS	... ...	£1 1 0
LADIES	... ...	. 10 6
FAMILY	... ...	1 10 0

Green Fees: 1/- per round.

The Green Keeper will give Lessons by arrangement.

TOM CARR, Hon. Treasurer.

Opening of the Newbury District Golf Club.

SATURDAY, JUNE 2nd, 1923.

MESSRS.

BRAID, RAY, SHERLOCK and TURNER

WILL OPEN THE ABOVE CLUB BY PLAYING A MEDAL ROUND,

starting at 11 a.m. on Saturday, June 2nd, to be followed by a FOUR-BALL MATCH in the Afternoon.

Charge for Admission to the Course: To Members and others, 2s. (tax included).

Luncheons, Teas and Refreshments will be obtainable on the Course.

THE COURSE WILL BE OPEN FOR MEMBERS FOR PLAY THE FOLLOWING DAY, JUNE 3rd, 1923.

It was pointed out that since work had ceased on the course, the fairway had become considerably overgrown, the greens had mostly become unrecognisable as such, new implements and paraphernalia were needed, so that the initial expenses of restarting the club and getting the links in a fair playing condition would be heavy. Mr. Witherby thought that at least £300 would be required for this purpose. At any rate, the consensus of opinion was that the club should be re-formed, and a resolution to that effect was unanimously agreed to. The meeting also was unanimous in the election of Mr. A.S.B. Tull as president, and Mr. A.G. Witherby as vice-president, Mr. John Louch as hon. secretary, and Mr. J. Greenshields as hon. treasurer.

A Provisional Committee, consisting of the old members present, and Mr. H.R. Metcalf and Mr. E.P. Plenty was chosen to go into the matter of the initial expense of re-starting the links and what the annual cost of running them under present day conditions would be. It was understood that Clinch would be the professional, and he, the President, the Vice-President, and the Committee surveyed the course yesterday (Wednesday) afternoon to see what was necessary to be done. A further meeting is to be called at the Guildhall Club at 6.30 on Monday, March 29th, when it is hoped that all golfers and intending members will be present, for at this meeting the committee will report as to what is necessary to be done, and give an estimate of the cost. Meanwhile Clinch is going to proceed with the work, so that no time shall be lost.

A member of the committee who went round the course yesterday afternoon informs us that the expense which must be incurred to get it in condition will necessarily be considerable, and that Mr. Witherby's estimate is, if anything, likely to be exceeded. A suggestion has been thrown out that one way of meeting this would be election of life members, and if there are any who would help in this way, or by giving donations, the Committee would be glad if they would communicate with Mr. Greenshields at the London, City and Midland Bank. At any rate, they hope there will be a large attendance at the adjourned meeting, and that those who are unable to come will send a postcard to the Secretary signifying their intention of joining the club.

Newbury Weekly News April 20th 1920

The adjourned meeting, called to report progress as to the resuscitation of the Crookham Golf Club, took place on Monday evening in the Lecture Room at the Guildhall Club, which had been kindly lent for the occasion. Mr. A.S.B. Tull, the Lord of the Manor of Crookham, presided, and referred to the work which had been done since the last meeting. He said that Clinch and two men were being employed getting the links in order, the cost in labour alone being £30 a month. The idea was to get nine holes ready for play by the first of June, and to proceed with the completion of the course after that date. It was necessary to secure members as early as possible, and also to raise a guarantee fund to meet the expense.

The question of the amount of the annual subscription was discussed, and it was decided that this should be three guineas a year, with a guinea entrance fee for members; two guineas and a guinea entrance for ladies, and family tickets, not exceeding four in family, seven guineas a year and three guineas entrance fee. In each instance, in the case of those joining before June 1st, the entrance fee will be remitted. A start was also made with the guarantee fund, several of those in the room putting themselves down for £5.

Play will be possible on a few holes almost immediately and the nine holes will be in good order by the first of June. The hon. secretary of the club is Mr. John Louch, of

Newbury, and the hon. treasurer, Mr. J. Greenshields, manager of the local branch of the London, City and Midland Bank.

We would throw out the suggestion that with the idea of popularising the club, a couple of well-known professionals should be secured for the opening day to give an exhibition round.

Newbury Weekly News November 11th 1920

This old-established club, which was re-formed in the spring of the year, made an encouraging start with its competitions on Saturday, October 30th, when the weather could not have been more favourable. Eight took part in the medal round, which was won by E.A. Marlow, handicap 2, with a net score of 85; Maurice Wells, scratch, 90; and F.H. Floyd, handicap 12, 90, tieing for second place. There were 16 starters in the bogey competition in the afternoon, and the winner was W.K.T. Hope, two down, the popular hon. secretary, J. Trevelyan Louch, who was five down, being second. The winner of the medal round is a signal-man at Midgham Station. The play in the afternoon in the bogey competition was rather disappointing, as no one seemed right on their game. The scores, both morning and afternoon, were not as good as usual in previous events. The course had been extended to its utmost length, which increased the par by two or three strokes, and added to its natural difficulties, which are pretty formidable, unless one keeps dead straight. It is hoped that the number of entries in subsequent events will be improved upon. The monthly medal competitions (18 holes under handicap) have again been started, and players can take out as many cards as they like during the month on payment of 1s. for each round and 2d. each for the cards. Players as yet having no handicaps are requested to put in three cards as soon as possible.

The opening of Newbury District Golf Club in June 1923 was a crucial blow to Crookham, and the decision to introduce artisan membership was probably the saving factor. There is no doubt that the uniqueness of Crookham and its place in golf history gave much pride to its members, but a new golf course sculptured in more interesting terrain, with all the requirements of modern golf was a threat to its existence, to which it reacted fairly successfully.

The AGM, June 1922, brought changes in the general aims and attitude of the club:

A resolution was passed which it is hoped will cause considerable interest in the game, to the effect that artisans, working in the neighbourhood, may be admitted as full members of the club at the annual subscription of half a guinea. This should enable many working men to find that the pleasures of the game of golf are not barred to them on the grounds of expense.

This was a bold attempt to counter the effects of the proposed new Newbury District Golf Club. It is probable that rumours were already spreading through the club regarding the formation of another course barely one mile away.

Crookham decided to reduce subscriptions:

Annual subs	2 guineas
Family ticket	3 guineas
Ladies subs	$1^1/_2$ guineas
Green fees to be	2/6 per day
	1/6 per round

Clinch was the established professional, and since 1920 had been preparing the course. Mr Collins was enlisted as greenkeeper.

As an added incentive for monthly competitions, it was decided to give silver spoons to the winners.

With the continued support, and persuasion of the president, the Lord of the Manor, Mr A.S.B. Tull, some golf was played at Crookham throughout 1923. How deserted and sombre was the Volunteer Inn on June 2nd, the opening day of Newbury District Golf Club?

In the report of the AGM, April 1923, there is a reference to Crookham being the 'oldest local club', and quite naturally the meeting was preoccupied by the opening of Newbury District.

The twelve months between the 1922 and 1923 AGMs must have been very confusing for all concerned with golf at Crookham, for although its future was plotted in 1922, it is strange to read in the 1923 report that "a resolution was unanimously and enthusiastically carried, that the Crookham Golf Club should be restarted. Messrs H. Lambdon and E. Povey were appointed as joint secretaries".

Mr Tom Carr the retiring secretary, became treasurer and the committee members elected were Messrs T. Moore, C. Thompson, C. Povey, T. Pollard and G. Bailey.

More confusion is caused by the last item in the report which states that "...arrangements have already been made to secure a greenkeeper who would give lessons if required .... The promoters are quite pleased with the result of the meeting, as the membership has reached 40". It was only one year earlier that they had announced the retainment of Clinch – and it is Clinch who features from this time forward.

Wally Clinch (1880-1963)

Walter Edwin Clinch lived within a few yards of The Volunteer Inn, the Crookham headquarters, and as mentioned earlier caddied for J.H. Taylor

---

Newbury Weekly News August 19th 1923
> The Crookham Golf Club would be very glad if any information could be obtained as to the whereabouts of the silver Challenge Cup which was last played for in 1915.

in 1894 at the age of 14. His progress was rapid and in 1897 he was appointed as professional – aged 17!

In 1899 he left to serve in the Boer War but following that there is no mention of him until the 1914-18 war when, according to his obituary, he served with the Royal Field Artillery.

His daughter in law, Mrs D. Clinch, who still lives in Newbury, speaks of Wally spending many of those lost years in Canada.

When Crookham reopened in 1920, Clinch was appointed as professional again, but the next ten years are as confusing to us as they must have been to him. He was seldom referred to as "professional" though regularly complimented upon his maintenance of the course. In club matches, as was

Wally Clinch in front of The Volunteer

the custom for club professionals in those days, he played at No 1 against the opponents professional, but from 1926 the name of F. Perkins appears playing in the No 1 position. Perkins had been the first professional at Newbury District in 1923, but had been dismissed in 1924. Without any evidence of an official appointment, Perkins seemed to assume the role of professional. Clinch at this time is recorded as participating in two club competitions i.e. a mixed foursomes and in the Crookham Challenge Cup – playing off a handicap of 3! When J.H. Taylor played at Crookham in 1929, Perkins played in the fourball game, with Clinch merely caddying for Taylor.

In 1930 there is a report which mentions that Clinch was "... now employed as their professional". Perkins is never mentioned again and Clinch was more evidently re-established as professional, naturally continuing with his groundsman duties. This situation remained until the course was lost. He was welcomed at Newbury District Golf Club until the amalgamation of the two clubs in 1946, and although his obituary in 1963 states that he was an honorary member of Newbury & Crookham, there are no records of this.

George Wathen

George Wathen was born in 1900, and at the age of 15 was sent to Sandhurst. He received a commission in the Royal Sussex Regiment, serving in the Army of Occupation in Cologne. He was later transferred to Ireland during the rebellion of 1922.

He came to the Newbury area in 1924 to learn poultry farming at Ball Hill, later starting his own business at Hawthorn's Poultry Farm, Tadley.

Wathen was playing golf at Bude, Cornwall at the age of seven, and was a plus handicap golfer when he arrived at Crookham and remained so for the six years he was there.

His obituary read:

> Mr Wathen was a fine golfer with a natural swing... he held the amateur record for Crookham, which he played in 64, six under bogey. By the quality of his hard work as Honorary Secretary (1929-30) and inspiring leadership as captain (1927), Wathen regained for Crookham the prestige formerly held in golfing circles. He increased its membership and was instrumental in getting the five times Open Champion J.H. Taylor to take an interest in the course, and thus considerably add to its popularity.
> He left in 1930 to take up the Secretaryship of the Seascale Golf Club, Cumberland, being appointed out of 200 applicants. In November 1932 he was appointed to a similar post at Knebworth, Hertfordshire.

Wathen set course records wherever he went. Those reported locally were: Crookham 1925, 1928 and 1929 (64, with only 19 putts), Great Salterns, Portsmouth 1930 and Seascale 1931.

He tied for the Berkshire County Stroke Play Championship in 1929, and lost in the final of the Cumberland Championship on his only attempt, in 1931.

Wathen tragically died of bronchial pneumonia early in 1933, aged 33. He had been playing golf the previous day, although he had been feeling unwell 24 hours earlier.

He was buried at Knebworth, overlooking the golf course. His putter, which was his favourite club, was buried with him. He left a widow, and three young children, the eldest being nine years old.

Mike Wathen, the younger of two sons, now plays at Westward Ho! and Saunton and remembers little of Crookham, but was able to produce the photographs of his father.

AGM April 1924

> The efforts made a year ago by Mr Tom Carr and others to reconstitute the Crookham Golf Club .... have met with gratifying success. A membership of 80 has been enrolled, most of whom are young players and are showing great keenness. There is now a balance in the bank of £2. Mr A.S.B. Tull is presenting a silver Challenge Cup".

The first winner of the Tull Cup in January 1925, was E.T. Povey who beat T. Carr 6 and 4.

Newbury Weekly News March 1926

> **Crookham Golf Club Dinner**
>
> Mr A.S.B. Tull was in the chair and guests included Mr C.W. Bloxsom (Hon. Sec. of Newbury District Golf Club) who brought with him a "feathery" golf ball dating from pre 1848 and a wooden putter which was won by his father 40 years earlier, which both proved of great interest[1].
>
> Others who sang were S. Lewis, Sid Stillman and A.F. Perkins, whilst Mr Bloxsom told humorous stories and Mr Gilbert recited.

Newbury Weekly News September 1926

> A new generation of golfers was seen on Crookham links on Saturday. They were scholars from Crookham School, whose ages range from nine to 13. A preliminary sort out took place on the first green where the boys and their headmaster, Mr Bliss, assembled.
>
> The leading scores in a twelve hole competition were:
>
> Douglas Collins 64, Donald Canning 71, Charlie Giles 73, Sidney Preston 74, Albert Tidbury 76, Douglas Aldridge 91, Douglas Allan 92, Reginald Cook 100.

Some evidence of the changing scene at Crookham came from Mr Broome Pinnegar who first played there in 1905, being honorary secretary/treasurer in 1908 – 1909.

He was a spectator at the final of the Crookham Handicap Cup in 1926, and he recalled then that in 1905 the fairways were much narrower, "with gorse bushes 12 feet high standing in the way". (He recalled also claiming a record by playing 27 consecutive rounds with the same ball).

Club finals in the 20s created great interest with large crowds in attendance, and hole by hole reports in the newspaper.

---

[1]This ball, in mint condition, is still in the possession of the family, and has been recently viewed by the author (1993)

The Course

In 1925 there had been much rejoicing when the Crookham Challenge Cup was recovered, having been lost since before the war.

> Enquiries were elicited near and far, search was instituted high and low. At length a casual remark bore fruit. The cup was remembered to have been submitted several years ago for engraving. A whole day's devotion to systematic search resulted in success, and the Cup, resting in its case, was brought to light. *Newbury Weekly News*

In an article in the local paper on June 17th 1926 it was announced that the Handicap Challenge Cup, presented to Crookham by Mr C. Stephens in 1874 had been recovered.

As both cups had been lost since before the war, there was great satisfaction for the present management to have these valuable links with the past recovered.

The report indicates that whoever was in possession of the Handicap Cup up to 1926 was owed money by the club: "Certain financial difficulties connected with the old club had to be overcome before possession could be obtained, and Mr Tom Carr, the present Chairman, has very generously met these and handed the Trophy over to the present club".

From 1874 the Crookham Challenge Cup had always been played for as a Scratch Trophy, but in 1926 it was changed to a handicap competition, and has remained so since as the Newbury & Crookham medal.

Newbury Weekly News March 1927
Crookham Club's Dinner
The annual dinner of the Crookham Golf Club took place on Friday last at the Cooper's Arms. Mr Tom Carr, the genial chairman of the club, presided in the regretted absence of Mr A.S.B. Tull, the president, who was unable to attend owing to a previous engagement. During the course of a very enjoyable evening, the Tull cup was presented to the winner, A.R. Wallin, and J. Steptoe paid the usual forfeit, an encore it is feared, for doing the 11th hole in one. Songs were contributed by Messrs S. Lewis and S.J. Stillman in their usual delightful manner, and the members excelled themselves in the rollicking choruses of the sea shanties and other old-time favourites.

J. H. Taylor Returns

In 1893, J.H. Taylor visited Crookham, when professional at Winchester. By the time he returned in 1929, he had become one of the most famous golfers, forming the triumvirate of Taylor, Braid and Vardon and, having won five Open Championships, possibly deprived of more by the First World War.

1926 Rules .... onus on fixing dates of matches rests on side with highest handicaps.

Wathen and Taylor

George Wathen was instrumental in bringing Taylor to Crookham. It was, however, of special interest to Taylor to return, as Crookham was by this time catering for artisans and Taylor himself had been a founder of the Artisan Association.

In 1893, W.E. Clinch had caddied for Taylor and he did so again in 1929. An exhibition match was played between Wathen and Taylor in the afternoon, which was followed by tea. On behalf of the Club, Taylor was asked to accept honorary life membership, which he did.

After tea a fourball was played between Taylor and G. Riches (Newbury District) and Wathen and F. Perkins, which was again followed by a large crowd.

Following his visit, J.H. Taylor donated a grand silver cup, later to be awarded to the winner of an annual Matchplay Competition, off handicap.

This cup is now used as one of the Foursomes Cups at Newbury & Crookham, the other being The Tull Cup (or President's Cup) both being handed over at the time of the merger in 1946.

Newbury Weekly News July 4th 1929

J.H. Taylor Describes Crookham Course

J.H. Taylor, five times open champion, was evidently much impressed by his recent visit to the Crookham Club, for he has written the following interesting article on the course in the News of the World under the title of "Where the game can be played as in the old days": Recently I renewed acquaintance with a course that took back my memory what appeared to be a very long time, but which in reality was only 36 years. It was long enough, at all events, to make me realise the great changes that have come over the game in the intervening years, both in its playing and in its conditions. The course to which I refer is that of the Crookham Golf Club, perched high on Crookham Common, near Newbury. Crookham is one of the very few courses that remain to remind us of the fact that our fathers were not so fastidious as we, and were quite content to obtain their pleasure in a humble fashion, bereft of those attributes that spell munificence.

Retains its Old Characteristics

Founded in 1873, it is one of the oldest golf clubs in the country. I made its acquaintance first in 1893, at a time when I had been but two years a professional. I still remember that I considered it a very difficult course, and even in those days somewhat rough and unkempt if judged by the standard – certainly not a high one – that existed then. On the occasion of my last visit, I was agreeably surprised and pleased to find that the course was almost exactly the same as it was 36 years ago, a tribute to the fact that the present users of it have not been obsessed by the march of golfing progress, but are as content to play upon it as in the days of the gutty ball, the leather-faced, long-shaped beech heads, spliced on to delicately-tapered and whippy shafts, finished off with thick leather grips nearly the size of cricket bat handles. The course is of full 18 holes, total length somewhere in the neighbourhood of 5,000 yards, and the greens, I imagine, were fixed upon because there happened to be clear spaces whereon they could be made, with the architect not concerned about the length that constituted a good two-shotter. This was a craze that was to come later, of which he was in blissful, and blessed, ignorance.

A Course All Golfers Should Visit

The reader must not be too eager to assume that because of its lack of length the course must of necessity be easy. He or she may take it from me that it is not. It offers a wide variety of strokes, which must be accurately played if it is to be covered in anything like par figures. The membership of the club is drawn from local residents, which, it is good to know include the tradesmen and artisans of the district, who are filled with a great pride. My caddie was the same person who carried my clubs as a small boy 36 years ago, which, I think, proves the great interest he has given to the game in the long interval. The kindly and thoughtful act I received as a great compliment. I am not ashamed to acknowledge that my object in writing this is to induce more golfers to visit and enjoy the type of golf to be obtained in this delightful spot – a type common to all many years ago, before courses became "shaved and shampooed", as is customary now. They may be assured of the heartiest of welcomes, and I am sanguine enough to think that they will thank me for the information.

In the period from 1920 – 1930 the following members supported the Crookham functions and competitions, first appearing in the year shown.

GENTLEMEN

1920
A.S.B. Tull
A.G. Wetherby
John Louch
J. Greenshields
H.R. Metcalf
E.P. Plenty
M.O. Wells
E.A. Marlow
W.K.T. Hope

1923
Gifford Wells
H. Lambden
Tom Carr
C. Thompson
C. Povey
T. Pollard
G. Bailey
E.T. Povey
L. Moore
G.F. Morton

LADIES
1928
Mrs. C.L. Wathen
Miss W.A. Humphries

1929
Mrs Powys-Lybbe
Miss P. Powys-Lybbe

1925
E. Coward
H.C. Smith
E. Tiley
J. Steptoe
G. Coward
J. Botsford
H. Suter
T. Pollard
W. Smith
S. Lewis
S. Stembridge
C. Leader
J. Buckland
P. Bailey
J. Robbins
M. Shave
H. Jones
S. Jacobs
J. Nicholson
H. Humphries

1927
S.J. Stillman

1928
H. Millett
J. Whiting
C. Redmond
J. Hill
H. Whiteman
T. Goodall
H. Randall
S. Dell

1929
J. Robbins
W. Church
H. Marlowe
S. Butters
J. Flook
H. Flook
R. Woods
W. Hazell
A.A. Woods
T. Barnes
W.G. Hopkins
E. Spence
R. Brindley
H. Marlow
N. Tredennick
T. Devinish
G. Parker
B. Whincup
H. Taylor

4

The Final Years 1930 – 1946

I t is ironic, and sad, to realise that in its last decade, Crookham was stronger than at any previous period of its history, with membership increasing annually and the arrival of several new trophies filling its calendar. The shackles of the past, when there had been only the two major trophies to play for, were finally broken. There were now full fixture lists for men's and ladies' matches and, of course, the most significant difference between the old Crookham, and the new, was club life itself.

Instead of a titled and upper class membership, there was now a mixture of local businessmen and artisans, although it is interesting to note that, although the development of artisan membership seemed to be a leading factor in the survival of Crookham in 1923, it was never again mentioned after the visit of J.H. Taylor in 1929. In 1931 the subscriptions were raised by 5 shillings, an increase of nearly 25%, making the men's subscription 26 shillings, described then as "the cheapest golf in England".

Newbury Weekly News Club Dinner 1930

Mr E.F. Spence KC, proposing the toast of "The Ladies", said he had retired from the bar in order not to make any more speeches, and here he was, making a speech without even receiving a fee (laughter). He really could not understand why he had been asked to propose the toast of "The Ladies", unless it was because he was the most antique golfer present. He was a golfer long before the club was formed, as he had played golf at Hoylake as long ago as 1868 [1] – but had not played between that date and 1912.

However he felt he got much more golf in going round in 120 shots than Mr Wathen did in going round in 68 (laughter). He also got more enjoyment as if Mr Wathen played two bad shots he probably went home and murdered half a dozen pullets.

Newbury Weekly News May 8th 1930

Incident Puts Result in Doubt

This year's competition for the historic Crookham handicap Challenge Cup of 1874 took place during the past week-end, being in the form of 36 holes medal play. Some splendid scores were returned, but owing to an unfortunate incident which occurred to one of the players in the first round, the result cannot be determined until a decision has been received from the County Union Committee.

[1]Surprising, as golf at Hoylake was first recorded in 1869.

The player concerned was L. Moore, who returned a net score of 135 for the 36 holes, and at the 17th hole in the first round his drive travelled towards the hedge bounding the course. The players in front were looking for a ball in the field over the hedge, which is out of bounds, and they found a ball there which they imagined to have just been driven by Moore. One of the players walked out on to the course, waved to Moore intimating that he had picked up his ball out of bounds, and threw the ball on to the fairway. Moore not realising that his ball had been out of bounds and thinking that it had been merely picked out of the hedge, which is itself not out of bounds, accordingly "dropped", and, losing a stroke, played his third from alongside the hedge instead of going back to the tee and losing stroke and distance according to the out-of-bounds rule.

On reaching the 18th green he was told by the player in front that he had been out of bounds. Apparently the ball was also seen to go out of bounds by one or two other players. As it seemed difficult to give a definite ruling on the spot, owing to Moore being unaware that he was out-of-bounds, it was decided to refer the matter to the Berks, Bucks and Oxon Committee. (Len Moore was disqualified).

Lady Wins Crookham Challenge Cup

Once again, one of the two cups dating back to 1874 was in the news, in November 1930.

As previously mentioned, most Crookham competitions were open to men and women, and on this occasion, Miss Winifred Little won the Crookham Challenge Cup (now known as the Newbury & Crookham Medal) being the only lady to have ever done so.

"Win" Little married Len Moore in 1933. Len had arrived at Crookham as a 12 year-old when his father, Tom, and his mother, took over The Volunteer Inn in 1918, but he saw nothing of golf until the course was re-opened, following the war. As his home was then the Crookham clubhouse, he soon became one of the best players, and remained so until its demise.

Len and Win both joined Newbury & Crookham when the amalgamation took place in 1946, eventually living next door to Jack Hughes, by the 14th tee. Win, captain of Newbury & Crookham in 1947, and its lady president from 1981 to 1982, died in 1982.

Len still plays golf, often with his daughter Anne, now Mrs Thomas.

Anne has a wonderful record at Newbury & Crookham which is detailed in a later chapter.

Apart from the Spence Ladies Foursomes, started in 1929, there were no competitions solely for ladies before 1931. Golf had been dominated by men, although not to the exclusion of ladies, all competitions being open to either sex. Miss Win Little was the only lady to win a competition prior to 1931. By 1933 there were three cups being played for by the ladies section.

In 1931 there were 35 lady members, and the first ladies committee was formed consisting of the Misses M. Parker, M. Heather, W. Little, N. Spencer and D. Parker, with Miss M. Parker as the Hon. Ladies Secretary.

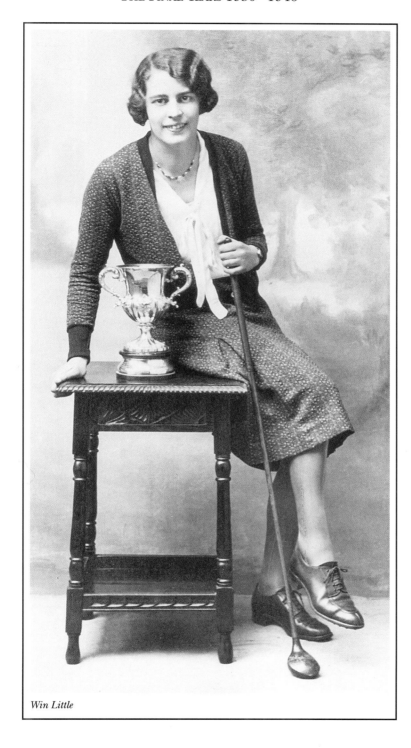

Win Little

The officers of the ladies section in the ensuing years were:

PRESIDENT	CAPTAIN	SECRETARY
1931-33 Miss M. Parker		
1933 Mrs E. M. Bramwell-Davis	Mrs H.I. Taylor	Miss M. Heather
1934 "	"	"
1935 "	"	"
1936 "	"	"
1937 "	Miss E. Wooff	Miss M. Heather/ Miss E. Wooff
1938 "	Mrs H. I. Taylor	Mrs H. Stradling

Mrs Evelyn Mary Bramwell Davis OBE, was the youngest daughter of Mr A.R. Tull, first president of Crookham.

She was president of Crookham Ladies from 1934 until 1938, the year of her death. In that year she had succeeded Mrs Lloyd H. Baxendale as president of Newbury District Ladies, but unfortunately died in office.

In 1934 she donated the Bramwell-Davis Cup, now used at Newbury & Crookham, with the Simonds Cup, as the Crookham Foursomes cups.

The Simonds Cup was donated jointly by the South Berks Brewery Co. Ltd, and Messrs H & G Simonds in 1929.

Wally Clinch on the converted De Dion Bouton tractor. The fairway drops away to the old Thatcham–Headley road in the background

Newbury Weekly News May 1932

Crookham AGM

The course had never been in better condition and Mr S. Stembridge (retiring secretary) had but one regret – that the scheme for the provision of a new clubhouse had not matured during his term of office.

Committee was elected as follows:

Joint Secretaries: H. Inman Taylor and B. Whincup

Treasurer: E.T. Povey;

Chairman: H.J. Humphries,

Captain: J.W. Hill.

Committee: S. Butters, T.E. Gunter, H.J. Humphries, J. Hill, G. Morton, J. Matthews, S. Stembridge, H.C. Suter, A.R. Wallen, and H.T. Whiteman. Miss D. Parker and Miss M. Parker were elected as joint secretaries of the ladies section and were empowered to form a ladies committee.

Newbury Weekly News January 26th 1933

Mrs Inman Taylor, Vice Captain of Crookham Ladies Golf Club holed her tee shot at the sixth hole, which is 150 yards, on Sunday last. The ball, after being driven was given up as lost, until another player discovered it lying in the hole.

So far as the records of the ancient club go, this is the first time a lady has holed in one at Crookham.

AGM May 4th 1933

The new standard scratch, allotted to the Club by the Union, was 67, which is a reduction in bogey of three shots. This meant that the 1st, 13th, 14th and 18th holes now become fours, and in order to retain the two fives they had to lengthen the third and 17th. There was thus an increase in the total length of 35 yards, bringing it to just under 5,000 yards.

This all means that individual handicaps must be adjusted, each to go up by three shots, but it was no discredit or disparagement.

In 1933, Messrs C. and T.E. Gunter presented the club with a new tractor mower, which was to transform the course. The correspondent in the *Newbury Weekly Years* described it with enthusiasm:

There is a sweetness and crispness about the turf which makes it glorious to play off.... It is a dinkie little outfit, and is so light that it will not mark the fairway even after the heaviest rain. Painted in green and red it looks as smart as it is adaptable. You would not guess its age, but the power unit is quite 20 years old.

It is a 6 h.p. De Dion Bouton, which does its work sweetly and without a murmur. Hitched on behind are two old pony cutters, which have been discarded since the war. It shows how engineering ingenuity and a lot of patience can provide a mower at a minimum of cost.

This is no fairy story, go and see it for yourselves and I think you will agree.

Also enthusiastic was the president, Mr A.S.B. Tull who was quoted in the report of the AGM:

Mr Tull proposed a hearty vote of thanks to Messrs Gunter who had fixed the Club up with a tractor. It had made all the difference to the Club, and they were now able to keep the fairways in good repair. The new outfit was a wonderful affair. It was painted green, with red wheels, and had Crookham Golf Club written all over it! (Laughter and applause).

Newbury Weekly News September 4th 1933

There was an exciting tussle in the third round of the Fourball Foursomes on Wednesday evening, and the headlights of motor cars had to be used to illuminate the course to enable the match to be completed.

J. Hill and H. Marlow were opposing C. Leader and C. Povey.

Setting out at 5.45, they were all square at the 15th, and then Povey won the 16th with a net four to put his side one up. The 17th was played in semi-darkness. Hill and Marlow won this hole and they went to the 18th all square.

They could then scarcely see the ball on the tee. Hill drove off first and had the satisfaction of hearing the ball drop in the middle of the fairway. The other three were not so lucky, for Marlow sliced his shot into the gorse and never saw it again, while Leader and Povey got into trouble in the heather in front of the tee.

It cost them three strokes to get on to the fairway. Povey soon lost his ball and so it was left to Leader and Hill to fight it out.

In the meantime members from the clubhouse came out to watch the exciting play, and a large number went on in front to help find the balls, and several cars switched on their headlights from all directions to illuminate the course.

Hill holed in six against Leader's eight, but as Leader received a stroke the excitement can well be imagined.

Newbury Weekly News October 12th 1933

With the dry weather, and the great run on the ball, some unusual holes have been done recently.

Captain Albon Bacon registered a two at the 14th which measures 386 yards. All that was necessary was a drive and a mashie shot. Captain Bacon who lives at The Malt House, Burghclere was a member of Crookham in pre-war days.

Then on Tuesday Sgt. Church of the Berks Constabulary did the sixth hole, 164 yards, in one.

This was only the third time that Sgt. Church had played golf. He has yet to appreciate its difficulties.

Newbury Weekly News Crookham AGM 1933

Several other matters were discussed among them that a portion of the road by The Volunteer Inn be treated with tarmac, as the gravel cuts golf balls driven on to it!

Newbury Weekly News 1934

On Sunday last a pleasing little ceremony took place when the "Jean" Cup, presented to the ladies by Mr H.E. Head, was handed to the winner, Miss N. Brown, by the donor's four year old daughter, Miss Jean Head.

New Clubhouse

From 1891 The Volunteer Inn had been the home of Crookham Golf Club, with always an excellent relationship between club, landlords, and brewers. Nevertheless since 1895 the club had nursed an ambition to build its own clubhouse. In particular the new wave of success of the 1930s meant that the single club room at the inn was inadequate.

In 1934, Crookham proudly opened the doors of its new "clubhouse", although it was built on to the side of The Volunteer Inn.

The landlords, H. & G. Simonds had built the new clubhouse which consisted of a large common room, ladies and men's changing room, and toilets.

> The building is of brick and timber, the front being entirely of local hand-made bricks. Inside the walls and ceilings are lined with patent wall boarding, finished in attractive panels. In the common room there are two large windows facing south, and two others with an east aspect. All of these give a picturesque panoramic view of the common and the course. On the walls are several water colours done for the original club by Mr A.G. Witherby, and a picture of J.H. Taylor, who is an honorary member of the club.

The official opening was attended by guests from Newbury District Golf Club, H. and G. Simonds, and Mr Oliver Brown of the firm of Love and Brown, the builders.

The president, Mr A.S.B. Tull was presented with a silver cigarette box, in acknowledgement of the tremendous support he had given to the project. Credit was also given to Mr B. Whincup who had carried through the details of the scheme.

The 1st hole at Crookham in the early 1930s

We now realise the irony of the story – there being barely six years remaining in the active life of the club.

Club life was normal well into 1939, when the most noteworthy event was the sale of the Crookham House estate. The house, built by Richard Tull in 1790 was sold to the Great Western Railway Company for use as offices. In more recent years, until 1991, it was the home of Crookham Court School, which ended in infamy and scandal. It is now let as flats.

Mrs Evelyn Mary Bramwell Davies OBE was the youngest daughter of Mr A.R. Tull, first president of Crookham.

She was president of Crookham Ladies from 1934 until 1938, the year of her death.

In that year she had succeeded Mrs Lloyd H. Baxendale as president of Newbury District Ladies, but unfortunately died in office.

In 1934 she donated the Bramwell-Davies Cup, now used at Newbury and Crookham, with the Simonds Cup for Crookham Foursomes.

The Simonds Cup was donated jointly by the South Berks Brewery Co. Ltd, and Messrs H. and G. Simonds in 1929.

Having survived the traumas of the early 1920s, Crookham had developed its course to a standard which compared well with that of the Newbury District Club, yet retained its own unique qualities.

The 1930s was a decade of growth and success, made possible by the influence of George Wathen. There was an increasing membership, including a thriving ladies section, challenging for many new trophies.

Club teams were strong, with low handicap players such as W.K.T. Hope, Len Moore, Jack Whiting and H. Marlow.

The last organised golf was played at Crookham in 1940. Shortly afterwards the Ministry of Defence requisitioned Greenham and Crookham Commons under emergency powers, for use as an airfield. The Newbury District Club generously opened its doors to Crookham members, with an arrangement intended to accommodate them for the duration of the war, but when the war ended the land was not released.

The Ministry of Defence explains that at the end of a period of requisitioning, land was either de-requisitioned and returned to the rightful owners or, as in this case, purchased because a continued requirement existed. Although the commons were not purchased until 1950, it became obvious in 1946 that there was no future for Crookham Golf Club. The Volunteer Inn, and the new clubhouse, had been demolished, and little remained of the course.

It was then that the Newbury District Golf Club generously offered the merger of the two clubs, and Newbury & Crookham Golf Club was born.

EASTER BOGEY COMPETITION — SIX INCHES — **16.**

CROOKHAM GOLF CLUB SCORE CARD

Name of Player

Date........................

Strokes received ....

Handicap ....

No of Hole	Name	Length in Yards	Stand'd Scratch Score	Strokes taken at	Player's Score	Oppo'ts Score	Result + — or 0	No. of Hole	Name	Length in Yards	Stand'd Scratch Score	Strokes taken at	Player's Score	Oppo'ts Score	Result + — or 0
1	Heather	374	4	6				10	Trap	164	3	12			
2	Sloper	157	3	17				11	Side Path	232	4	16			
3	Whin	430	5	2				12	Lawn	198	3	13			
4	Straits	340	4	7				13	Dard'nel's	367	4	5			
5	Avenue	263	4	11				14	Gorse	386	4	1			
6	Ha ha	394	4	4				15	Pond	129	3	18			
7	Lodge	195	3	14				16	Gate	290	4	10			
8	Tree Loft	230	4	15				17	Open	425	5	3			
9	Angle	194	3	9				18	End	370	4	8			
		2577	34	Out						2561	34	Home			

AGAINST S.S.S.		
Holes	Up	Down

Strokes taken in match play or against S.S.S. where the number in Red is equal to or less than the number received.

Out ....

Gross Total ...

Less Handicap

Nett Total ...

Signature of Marker ....

Crookham Card 1930. Note the 6" stymie measure

PRESIDENT
1874-1880	A.R. Tull
1891-1897	W.G. Mount
1898-1914	A.R. Tull
1920-1946	A.S.B. Tull

CHAIRMAN
1924-1930	T. Carr
1931	T. Carr/H.J. Humphries
1932-1938	H.J. Humphries

SECRETARY/TREASURER
1874-1875	Capt. R. Dashwood Fowler
1876-1880	Mr. C. Stephens
1891-1899	Rev. H.H. Skrine
1900-1904	C.H.H. Macartney
1905-1907	E. Fowler
1908-1909	Broome Pinnegar
1910-1914	L.V. Lodge
1922	T. Carr

SECRETARY
1923	H.Lamdin/E.Povey
1924-1925	H. Lamdin
1926-1928	J.E. Robbins
1929-1930	G. Wathen
1931	B. Whincup
1932-1936	H. Inman Taylor
1937-1940	W.H. Davies

TREASURER
1922-1923	T. Carr
1924-1946	E.T. Povey

PROFESSIONAL
1874-1875	T. Manzie
1895-1897	G. Founds
1898-1899	W.E. Clinch
1919-1940	W.E. Clinch

GROUNDSMAN
1891	Marsh/A.S. Denness
1892-1894	A.S. Denness
1895-1900	G.W. Millsom
1903-1914	F. Dodd
1919-1940	W.E. Clinch

CAPTAINS
1892-1893	A.H. Evans
1894	A.C. Bartholomew
1895	A.B. Cooke
1896	Rev. J. Stewart
1926	H.C. Suter
1927-1930	G. Wathen
1931-1945	J.W. Hill

COURSE RECORDS
1892	A.B. Cooke	90
1893	A.B. Cooke	78
1898	W.E. Clinch	71
1928	G. Wathen	65
1929	G. Wathen	64
1933	J. Hughes	64

HANDICAP CHALLENGE CUP
(Now Newbury & Crookham Bogey)

1926	H.E. Collins
1927	A. Gibbs
1928	J. Matthews
1929	F.C. Buckland
1930	J. Hazell
1932	A. Burridge
1933	J. Whiting
1934	H.W. Hillman
1935	J. Whiting
1936	Vice-Admiral D.C.F. Moir
1937	L. Moore
1938	V. Rummins
1939	J. Whiting

CHALLENGE CUP
(Now Newbury & Crookham Medal)

1926	G.W.D. Wathen
1927	E.T. Povey
1928	G.W.D. Wathen
1929	S. Stembridge
1930	Miss W. Little
1931	A. Gibb
1932	F.J. Whiting
1933	R. Ursell
1934	W.B. Wilson
1935	J. Whiting
1936	B.J. Yarr
1938	A.A. Jones

CROOKHAM MIXED FOURSOMES

1934	R.F. Cook, Miss B. Flook
1935	H. Humphries, Miss W. Heather
1937	Miss Wooff, A. Wilson
1938	L. Moore, Mrs J. Whiting

BRAMWELL DAVIS CUP

1933	Miss Heather
1934	Miss B. Flook
1935	Miss Flook or Miss Heather
1936	Miss Wooff
1937	Miss Wooff
1938	Mrs. H. Stradling

TULL CUP
(These are now awarded for Newbury & Crookham
             Foursomes)

1925 E. Povey
1926 G.D. Wathen
1927 A.E. Wallin
1928 G.D. Wathen
1929 S. Stembridge
1930 G.D. Wathen
1931 J. Hazell
1932 D.E. Gunter
1933 Miss Heather
1934 E.T. Povey
1935 E.T. Povey
1936 F.J. Flook
1938 R. Morrison
1939 J.A. Dean

SPENCE FOURSOMES
1929 S. Butters, A. Wallin
1930 Miss Little, S.W. Butters
1931 H.I. Taylor, B. Whincup
1933 J.H. Miller, W. Wilson

J.H. TAYLOR CUP

1929 F. Brindley
1930 J.W. Hill
1931 A. Gibbs
1933 J.A. Dean
1934 L. Moore
1935 A. Gibbs
1936 B.J. Yarr
1938 R. Morrison

SIMMONDS CUP
1929 T.E. Gunter
1930 S. Stembridge
(after 1930, Ladies only)
1931 E.M. Pearce
1932 Miss M. Heather
1933 Miss Heather
1934 Miss E. Wooff
1935 Miss M. Heather
1936 Mrs. J. Whiting
1937 Miss E. Wooff
1938 Mrs C.R. Leader
1939 Mrs Wasey
1940 Mrs C.R. Leader

CROOKHAM FOURSOMES

1925 P. Bailey, J.E. Robbins
1927 E.T. Povey, T. Carr
1928 Mrs G. Wathen, Miss Humphries
1929 A. Gibbs, J. Matthews
1930 Gunter/Gunter or
        G.Wathen/Butters
1932 S. Widdicombe, J.B. Lee
1934 E.T. Povey, J. Hazell
1935 J.W. Hill, J. Whiting
1936 S.A. Miller, D. Gunter
1938 J. Whiting, L. Moore

LADIES FOURSOMES
1935 Miss M. Heather, Mrs Moir
1937 Mrs Wooff, Miss Openshaw

JEAN CUP
1934 Miss W. Brown
1936 Mrs Ursell
1937 Miss M. Heather

Part II

Newbury District Golf Club

Colonel J.A. Fairhurst

Previous page. The Clubhouse 1923 - The Opening Day
The building on the left was the men's changing rooms. This protruded further than the replacement building which is now the secretary's office. The separate building to the right was the professional's shop, which was constructed with old ammunition boxes and wire netting from the 1914-18 war. It was demolished in 1963

5

The Founding 1923 – 1930

In 1922 a syndicate was formed by Colonel J.A. Fairhurst to support the construction of the new golf course and then to oversee the affairs of the proposed golf club.

The original "Proprietary Syndicate" members were: Colonel J.A. Fairhurst, who lived at Arlington Manor, now the home of Mary Hare Grammar School, Mr Lloyd H. Baxendale, Lord of the Manor of Greenham, living at Greenham Lodge, Mr Armah Saunderson, Colonel E.A. Stanton and Mr Raynor.

Colonel Fairhurst had already arranged with Mr Baxendale for the lease of 120 acres of the parkland surrounding the Lodge. In addition, included in the lease, were the buildings used as laundry and stables to the Lodge, to be used as the clubhouse. The same buildings, with additions and adjustments are still in use.

The experts engaged to plan and supervise the construction were professionals James Sherlock and John H. Turner.

James Sherlock was first engaged as a professional at Oxford University before moving to Stoke Poges and, by 1922, to Hunstanton. His best performances in the Open Championship were 6th at Sandwich in 1904 and 8th at St Andrews in 1905. He was a frequent winner of professional tournaments.

John H. Turner was formerly engaged at RMC Camberley, Thornock, Gainsborough, Flackwell Heath, Denham, and, by 1922, Frilford Heath. His contribution was by far the greater, being responsible for most of the design of the course.

Also imported was W. Field, the Frilford Heath greenkeeper, who supervised the construction. Upon its completion, Field remained at Newbury as the first Club Steward.

When the new course was ready, the greenkeeping was temporarily carried out by Dalby, the head gardener of Mr Baxendale at Greenham Lodge (Dalby being later "immortalised" by having Dalby Crescent named after him).

It was estimated that the new course would cost more than £2,000, and life memberships were offered at £50 each, to which there was an excellent response, and this, together with considerable contributions from Colonel Fairhurst had made the project viable. In 1946 there were still 15 surviving life members, from the original 27, the last being Colonel Stanton. All the plans and arrangements so far described were carried out by the Syndicate, steered by Colonel Fairhurst, who was well supported by Colonel Stanton, who was acting as Secretary. The course was completed, appointments made, and an exhibition match arranged for an official opening, before the first meeting of the club was held.

One of the early appointments made was the professional F.S. Perkins who came from the Chatham United Services Course. While in the Royal Marines he had played golf around the world and been champion of the Navy.

Appointed by Perkins, before the course was opened, was a young assistant for the pro shop. His name was Jack Hughes.

On May 24th 1923 an exhibition featuring James Braid, Edward Ray, James Sherlock and John H. Turner was held.

The exhibition match was a success, the imposing figure of James Braid of Walton Heath being the great attraction. His record in The Open Championship was: Champion in 1901, 1905, 1906, 1908 and 1910. He was also second in 1909 and third in 1902, 1904 and 1912. Braid was 53 and his best performances were behind him.

Edward Ray from Oxhey Golf Club was seven years younger than Braid and only three years earlier had been second in the Open. His Open record was: champion in 1912, second in 1913 and 1920, third in 1908 and 1925. He had also won the U.S. Open.

Making up the fourball were Sherlock and Turner who, together with Ray were partners in the business of golf architecture.

A significant difference between the course then and now was that the 14th was a par 5 of 490 yards, the green being further on, well beyond the present green. The hole did not impress Braid who, when taking stance remarked "Now for the straight mile", giving the hole its title for many years to come. The 15th was then a short par 4.

Braid was greatly impressed with the course and Ray praised Turner for his design of many beautiful holes.

The card is reproduced with present day yardage shown for comparison.

	(Now)							
1.		380	(399)	10.	(8)	425	(428)
2.	(11)	350	(357)	11.	(9)	180	(175)
3.	(12)	265	(289)	12.	(10)	270	(336)
4.	(2)	270	(288)	13.		400	(493)
5.	(3)	130	(161)	14.		490	(410)
6.	(4)	375	(381)	15.		285	(206)
7.	(5)	360	(352)	16.		410	(394)
8.	(6)	140	(124)	17.		130	(164)
9.	(7)	420	(465)	18.		405	(458)
Length 1923		5685					
Length 1994		5880					

Being a new course, there were problems, especially as a high percentage of the members were new golfers. *The Newbury Weekly News* added a significant paragraph at the end of its report on the exhibition match.

> Generally speaking the rough has claimed more than its share of victims. There has been an orgy of ball losing. The classic case is that of one member who went out with ten balls, he played eight holes and then returned to the clubhouse as he had no more left. Another member and his wife disposed of a cool two dozen in three days. Another member, who is just taking up the game, evidently means to be prepared for eventualities for he has invested in a gross of balls.

By the end of June 1923, the membership was: Life Members 27, Men 154, Ladies 115, Juniors 19.

THE EXHIBITION MATCH

*Left to right: James Braid, James Sherlock, Ted Ray, Col.Stanton, Jack Turner, Col.Fairhurst,
Field (steward), F.S.Perkins (professional)*

The 5th green (3rd)

MAY 24th 1923

The 6th tee (4th)

The 8th green (6th)

Hugh Turner, Editor of the Newbury Weekly News, used photographs of the exhibition match of 1923 in a handbook produced immediately after it, for which he wrote the text. His description of the course is reproduced in full with some of the accompanying advertisements

Newbury District Golf Club

BUILT for the big hearted golfer, Newbury was destined from the opening day to take its place among the best inland links in the country. There is nothing puny, cramped or artificial about it. Nature, rather than man, plays the predominant part in its lay out. Plateaus, ridges, and gullys have been boldly turned to account by its architect, with the result that the true golfer succumbs to its charms on first acquaintance. For he finds it a course to be conquered. He progresses but a very little way on his journey ere he realises that he is being tested the whole time and that an infinite variety of shots are needed to bring him safely home. But while careless and wild methods will assuredly lead to trouble, from which it is no use depending upon luck to escape, good shots will meet with their merited reward and bring with them the exhilaration of difficulties overcome.

While not more than a mile and a half from the town, the course might very well be in the heart of the country.

9

It stands on the uplands parallel with Greenham Common A glorious panorama stretches in front of you, bounded on the south by the Hampshire hills, the most prominent feature of which is the Beacon, on the summit of which is the Earl of Carnarvon's lonely grave. In the other direction, you look across the Kennet Valley, with the Racecourse lying at your feet. Whilst scenery is not golf, it is at least an attractive adjunct to those who have a little poetry in their souls as well as a desire to hole putts. The course possesses a charm of its own in its picturesqueness, for their is a wonderful change of scene as you proceed from hole to hole. The fifth is quite a gem both from a golfing and scenic standpoint. As you take your stance on the tee the green looks up at you 130 yards away in the gully beneath. To be properly appreciated it must be seen in spring time when on either side of the emerald-like green there is a gorgeous purple carpet formed of masses of blue bells, whilst a few weeks later its slopes are studded with gigantic foxgloves.

The course starts out in an easterly direction and the first hole calls for little comment, as it hardly gives the new-comer a taste of the quality which is in store for him. The second, however, is quite a sporting proposition, lying on the point of a hog's back. Unless the ball is kept rigidly to the spine of the hill, the slope insidiously draws it off its proper course, and the man who slices will sure

to have this accentuated with the prevailing wind from the south-west which blows right across the fairway. The front entrance to the green is guarded left and right with bunkers, and it is surrounded by a grassy hollow. The hole is 350 yards and the bogey five is on the generous side. Number three is a drive and a pitch, being but 265 yards in length, with a bunker in the front of the green in the direct line for the pin.

Now you come to a hole characteristic of the course. The way to the green lies across a yawning gully,

10

through a narrow pass which has been cut in a larch plantation, with a formidable bunker at the top of the gully on the left. A nicely hit tee shot comfortably reaches the fairway on the other side, but a sliced or pulled ball will ricochet amongst the larches. In the summer time also your approach will need careful judgment, as the green slopes away, which makes it very easy to over run, and so down a steep bank. The features of the short fifth have already been described. It calls for an accurate shot with a mashie or a mashie niblick, the ball having to be dropped "plonk" on the green, as in front of you is a deep gully with a ditch at the bottom, whilst if you get in the rough right or left you may get out with your second, but the chances are against you. The green which has been entirely carved out of the wood, has been worth the great labour it entailed, for it is one of the best on the course and the hole is artistic in its conception.

The sixth tee lies to the north of the fifth green, and the drive is over what was formerly a thick wood. It requires to be hit truly for there are several bits of boggy ground to be crossed which will trap the short one, whilst a slice takes you up amongst the trees on the right. The green is 375 yards away on the north east corner of the course in the direction of the starting gate for the straight mile on the Newbury Racecourse. The approach must be kept straight as there is only a narrow neck to the green which is surrounded by a grassy bank. Now we turn round and face up the hill in a southerly direction, and the player here will need to get his tee shot well away to carry the deep ditch which cuts across the fairway. The big hitter will sometimes reach and stay on the green in two, but more often he will not, and the ordinary player will require the bogey five to complete the hole. The green has been cut out of the hill side and made in a double wave which should prove an attraction to the canny putter.

The eighth hole has been named "Turner's Grave" after the Frilford Heath professional who laid out the course, and it necessitated the filling up of a gully for a considerable distance to a depth of some 10 or 12 feet. It is a one-shot hole, 140 yards in length, and the green is guarded on the front by a ravine and on the sides by several big bunkers. It you play straight for it the ravine is waiting to catch the ball that is short. The man with a slice who plays to the left may come off here, for the ground slopes down to the green from this side. The outward journey is completed with a nice open hole with a down-hill drive. It is slightly dogged-legged, and the approach is the critical shot for there is a ditch with running water either side of the entrance neck to the green. The hole measures 425 yards and the bogey is five.

The four most difficult holes on the course have next to be negotiated, and a mistake with either of them in your tee shot will seriously jeopardise a good score. The tenth causes more weeping and gnashing of teeth than any hole on the course. A feature lurking with danger for the unwary is the insidious stream which runs diagonally down the fair way. You must open your arms with your tee shot in order to carry the narrow waste where the wood has been cut down with your second shot. Woe betide you if you go astray with this.

A hook will take you into a boggy gully, whilst if you get a slice the chances are your ball will bound into the wood. The green itself lies half way up the hill, from which it has been hollowed out. After that comes a one-shot hole, 180 yards long, across the gully towards Greenham Lodge. Your tee shot must be of the best, for the broken ground runs right up to the Green and the wind is nearly always against you. Grief and pain awaits the man who is short, as bogs, stumps and ditches are ready to

trap his ball and make the second shot an uncertain quantity.

The way to the twelfth is back over the same gully in an easterly direction, the men's tee lying well back close to the green, whilst the ladies' is put forward on the edge of the gully. A good shot is required to reach the top of the further bank, to be followed by a well-directed mashie to find the green which is 270 yards from the tee. Another good tee shot is required for the thirteenth, for the gully has again to be crossed, this time in a westerly direction and it is a long carry. If you land in it the odds are your ball will be bogged. The green, which is 400 yards away, lies alongside the eighteenth and is banked up and surrounded by approach bunkers.

The next is the longest hole on the course, the "straight mile," as Braid called it when he was down for the opening. It is just on 500 yards in length, requires three nice shots to reach it, and when there the green will be found to be well pitched up with a ridge across the centre.

The fifteenth hole presents no great difficulties, with the exception that accuracy in direction is needed for the tee shot in order to miss the tree on the left, and the bunker on the right. There is a dog-leg hole for the sixteenth, with a drive over a moderate gully. The second is the crucial shot. The man who knows how to play with a pull can get within pitching distance of the green, otherwise a longer approach will be needed. The seventeenth is the shortest and one of the most difficult of the lot, for although the carry is small the road to the farm has to be crossed, whilst the green lies hedged about with bunkers on every side. The eighteenth is a straightforward one, the green lying alongside the thirteenth, not far from the Club House.

On the whole it is a long driver's course, but the ladies are liberally treated by their tees being well advanced.

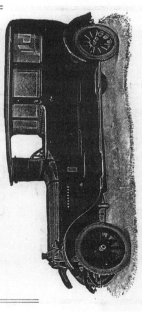

Inauguration

The first Annual General Meeting of the Newbury District Golf Club was held on June 11th 1923, and at the outset Lord Ronaldshay was elected as President.

Mr Fairhurst was elected Captain. In thanking the members he explained how the Syndicate had examined various sites in the district, and hopes were fading when they discovered the opportunity at Greenham.

Colonel Stanton and Commander England[1] were appointed as Joint Secretaries, and Mr J. Greenshields, Manager of the London Joint City and Midland Bank was elected Hon. Treasurer.

According to rules imposed by the Syndicate three members of the Committee were elected by the Syndicate and it was announced that they had nominated Mr Lloyd A. Baxendale, Colonel Stanton and Mr A. Saunderson. This left four members to be elected by the meeting. Major Tilney, W.H.T. Hope, M.O. Wells, and H. Turner were elected.

Subscriptions were boldly set at 5gns for men and 3gns for ladies, matching those of leading golf clubs. The first 200 men and 100 ladies were to pay no joining fee.

Some of the rules of the syndicate were:

1.   The club shall be called Newbury District Golf Club.
2.   The club is proprietary, the members having no liability beyond their subscriptions.
3.   The appointment of secretary and staff of the club shall be under the control of the proprietary syndicate, who are solely responsible for all expenditure. The appointment of secretary shall be subject to the approval of the committee appointed by the members.
4.   The management of the club shall be in the hands of a committee consisting of president, captain and seven members of whom three shall be nominated by the proprietary syndicate. Three to form a quorum. The proprietary syndicate shall have the power to veto any recommendation of the committee affecting the financial status of the club.
12.   If any member shall be made a bankrupt or shall make a public composition with his creditors, he shall, ipso facto, cease to be a member of the club.
23.   Ladies are permitted to be members of the club on the reduced subscription, but must be proposed and seconded by male members. Ladies shall take no part in the management of the club.
30.   In no case is a member of the staff or servant of the club to be reprimanded by a member

---

[1]Commander Richard Bruce England was born in 1883. He followed his father into the Royal Navy and served with Captain Beatty, later Admiral of the Fleet in China, being mentioned in despatches. During the 1914-1918 war he served on the destroyer *Conquest*, which was torpedoed in the Bay of Biscay. He was in the water for 16 hours before being picked up. He was awarded the DSO. He retired 1922, with the rank of captain.

In a separate meeting, the ladies section elected its officers – lady president, Mrs Baxendale; captain, Mrs Douglas of Hazelby; hon. secretary, Miss Muirhead of Baughurst. Committee members: The Hon. Mrs Saunderson, Miss Kitcat, Miss MacDougal, Mrs Bramwell Davis and Mrs Stanton.

New Professional

Perkins had proved himself an excellent golfer, regularly lowering his record scores for the course, finally to 68. Unfortunately he did not suit the club well in other respects, and was released after just one year. As shown in the Crookham Golf Club history, Perkins stayed on in the area for several more years.

In October 1924, the replacement professional was George Riches who had worked under his uncle, Len Holland, at Northampton for $2^1/_2$ years. Riches settled in well, being a good player and clubmaker. These were still the days of hickory shafts and there was much work for a professional in repairing and making clubs.

Prior to the change of professionals, in 1924, Alec Kirkpatrick arrived as greenkeeper. He was the son of the greenkeeper at Rye, and had been brought up on the course. Although showered with praise for a few years, by 1927 there were rumblings of discontent and Kirkpatrick was suddenly given his notice. The intention was to have Riches combine the duty of professional with that of supervising the greenkeeping. He accepted this responsibility with no immediate increase in wages.

Mr E.H. Bance recommended Sgt-Major Whitlock for the new position of foreman on the course to the committee, and he was employed at 52 shillings per week. Whitlock's daughter, Mrs Pat Fidler, remembers being given rides over the course and is also able to boast a relationship to F. Dodd, greenkeeper at Crookham for many years from 1900. Her husband was Dodd's grandson.

New Cups

The Captain's Cup was given by Colonel Fairhurst, in 1924 and was then, as now, played over 36 holes, off handicap. The original condition stated that it should become the property of any member winning it three times.

The Elkington Cup was donated by Lieut-Col. J.F. Elkington DSO, in 1924 for matchplay, off handicap, for which it was used until 1985, when it became the scratch matchplay championship.

The Fourball Cups were presented jointly, in 1925, by W.K.T. Hope, J.T. Louch and Dr T.G. Starkey Smith.

The Ronaldshay Cup was presented by the president, the Earl of Ronaldshay (Marquis of Zetland), in 1925 for matchplay, off handicap.

M.O. Wells and C.W. Bloxsom also jointly gave a pair of cups for monthly foursomes, which have not survived.

Not to be outdone, the ladies section was soon playing for the following cups:

The Douglas Cup donated in 1925 by Mrs Cosmo Douglas, the first captain.

The Baxendale Cup, presented by the ladies' president, Mrs Lloyd H. Baxendale in 1924.

The Platt Cup followed in 1926. When the first ladies medal was played on December 11th 1923, there were ten entries. Miss Platt was the only one to break 100 with 96-11=85, winning 5 shillings in the sweep.

There was an intimate club atmosphere from the outset and social functions had a simplicity which would be impossible to repeat today.

Following the final of the Elkington Cup in 1924, a celebration dinner was held at the Hatchet Restaurant, where the trophy was presented to the winner H.D. Floyd, who had beaten Major Somerset Saunderson with a 4 at the 36th hole. After several complimentary toasts, Col. Fairhurst acted as host of a musical evening. The Colonel contributed his renowned coster and Irish songs. Mr Bloxsom performed several whistling solos and songs were also rendered by Messrs Gifford, Wells, Henry Saunderson and B. de Castro.

The course naturally needed time to settle down, and changes were made in the early years.

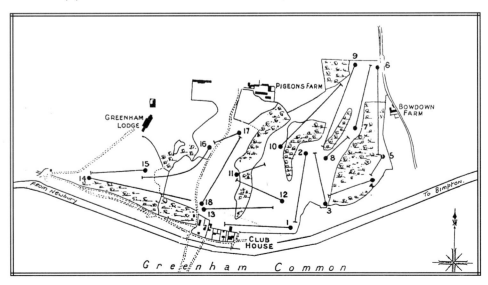

In September 1925, golf architect Tom Simpson visited Newbury and praised the design and quality of the course, remarking that he thought the 4th hole (2nd) was "a superb hole for tigers".

There was a change of secretary in January 1926 when Colonel England moved to Woolhampton, retired, and was replaced by Mr. C.W. Bloxsom and Mr J. Greenshields, who were to share the responsibility for the remainder of the year. Bloxsom then became secretary and remained so until 1942.

Also in 1926 two new cups were presented for annual competition. Major E.R. Portal, of Eddington, donated a cup to be played for as a "flag"[1] competition, at Easter. The silver cup was originally presented by him to Hungerford Golf Club, and it still bears the original engraving. As the Hungerford Club did not survive, Major Portal transferred his interest, and his cup, to Newbury. One of Major Portal's sons was Marshal of the RAF, Viscount Portal of Hungerford who was also chief of air staff from 1940 to 1945. Another son was Admiral Sir Reginald Henry Portal. Major Portal died in 1953.

Mr Frank Kirby, of Riverside, Donnington at the same time donated the Kirby Cup, a silver tankard. The two cups were played for at Easter until the early 1980s, when the Kirby Cup was moved to another date.

Frank Kirby was a "character for his period", as this article in the *Newbury Weekly News*, April 1926 illustrates:

> ....a performance which Mr. Frank Kirby did almost fortnightly as a mere matter of course is worthy of note. A year or so ago, when close on 60 years of age, living at Speen, he was a member of the Wallingford Board of Guardians. On meeting days he would start off from Speen on his push bicycle, ride to Wallingford, sit through the meeting, then ride back to Speen, and afterwards to the Newbury District Golf Club, finishing up with an 18 hole round. On these occasions he must have done 50 miles on his bicycle, before he played golf. Mr. Kirby is a refreshing person to meet in these days of luxurious locomotion. Although well over the half century mark, sometimes, when he went to Wallingford by train he would think nothing of making the return journey on foot.
>
> Thanks to an outdoor life, he is as hard as nails. At one time he was a trapper in the Hudson Bay territory.

Kirby was disqualified from the Captain's Cup (Fairhurst) in 1926 because he played an additional 18 holes between his first and second rounds in the competition. There was compensation when he won the trophy the following year. He died in 1929.

---

[1] The original description of a "flag" competition was a "Tombstone". So called to describe the pieces of paper pegged, as flags, into the fairway

Top row: M.O. Wells, W.K.T. Hope, N.T Tredinnick, Hugh Turner, Vernon Rivers, L.E. Yeomans
Sitting: S. Widdicombe, R.A. Angier, W. Smith.

In 1928, 36 hole challenge matches were played between the professional and senior amateurs of Crookham versus their counterparts from Newbury District. G. Wathen and Perkins, of Crookham, played M.O. Wells and Riches of Newbury, first at Henley where the Crookham pair won 5 and 4. The return match, played at Basingstoke, was won by Newbury 3 and 2. Wathen dominated both games, playing the second round at Henley in only 26 putts.

A letter was sent to all members in December 1927 informing them of the intention to drain all the lower fairways, at an estimated cost of £500, and asking for contributions towards this expense. Following this, an item appeared in the minutes for January 30th 1828:

> A letter was read from the landlord's (Baxendale) agents drawing attention to the shallowness of the new drains. As this letter was not written in terms requiring an acknowledgement, it was decided to leave it unacknowledged.
>
> It was proposed to draw the landlord's attention to the condition of the ditch running from the club to the 4th (2nd) tee.

By 1930 the club was firmly established and growing in stature. Minute books and press reports show, time and again the generosity of its members, in particular those on the committee.

Many of the everyday requirements in running the club were provided, or paid for, by individuals. By this time, however, some members, frustrated at being dominated by "The Syndicate" were showing discontent, and, at the AGM in July 1930, Mr Fairhurst read out the list of financial losses in the years since the club started: (1925 – £352; 1926 – £2; 1927 – £70; 1928 – £238; 1929 – £15.)

He also reminded members that the principle of the syndicate, as laid down, was that any profits made were to be put back into the club. The syndicate had made a loan of £2,000 to start the club, and interest owing on that was £600. At the time of addressing the members the club was overdrawn by £118 and total liabilities amounted to £2,800.

The syndicate had never given the membership any financial information, believing that it was their responsibility entirely. Now they realised that criticism, both of the club and the course, could have been avoided if the members had been made aware of the financial situation. From this time on there was more unity within the club, and renewed ambition for the future.

Later the balance sheet published for 1931 showed a profit.

Short Game

These "shots" are selected from various minute books, unless otherwise indicated.

1923

A letter from Perkins was read out and it was decided to conform to the normal practice and pay £10 for his removal to Newbury. He, when leaving to have to either pay his own expenses or arrange with his new employer.

*

The steward to be instructed to order in a new barrel of beer before the existing one runs out so that the beer may settle.

*

A report having been received that on Monday October 8 two ladies blocked two gentlemen players on the 9th (7th) green, when "fore" was shouted 3 times by the gentlemen under Bye-Law 6. No notice was taken by the ladies who continued to play on. One of the ladies, not a member, asked for one of the gentlemen's names whilst declining to give her own.

The Committee decided that a letter be sent to the secretary of the ladies' committee requesting that an explanation be furnished.[1]

A letter was read from the ladies' honorary secretary on behalf of the ladies' committee in reply to a communication sent to them by the last committee meeting stating that the ladies' committee had made an enquiry into the breach of bye-law 6 by two ladies on October 8th, and that the lady concerned had requested the ladies' committee to convey her apologies, and those of her guest to the club committee for the regrettable incident, and that the misunderstanding arose through confusion of Rule 3, Etiquette of Golf, with Bye-Law 6 of the Club.

The committee accepted the apology and desired that the ladies' committee be informed that they appreciate the manner in which their communication of October 11th had been met.

With reference to the latter part of the ladies' honorary secretary's letter, it was decided to point out that etiquette rule 3 of the Royal & Ancient Golf Club of St Andrews, and bye-law 6 of the Newbury & District Golf Club must be read in conjunction and that in cases where one match is overtaking another the bye-law would override the etiquette rule 3.

The object of bye-law 6 being to qualify rule 3 of etiquette in certain cases and that it must be obvious to the ladies' committee that if this were not so the bye-law could be negatory.

*

It was decided to authorise the captain, Mr Fairhurst to purchase a horse for the golf club to replace the horse kindly given by Mr Saunderson which was now becoming too old for the work required of it.

---

[1]The bye-law in question may be the one discovered in print in the early 1950s, which required that...ladies playing golf are to stand aside and let gentlemen through at the shout of "fore!"

1924

It was proposed by Mr A. Saunderson and seconded by Colonel Stanton that endeavours be made to get 500 to 600 sheep on the course, the club to pay the shepherd's wages.

*

It was decided that Ladies be allowed to play on Saturdays after 4 pm.

*

It was decided to make the penalty for driving out of bounds "loss of distance only".

*

Mr J.A. Fairhurst has presented the club with his old white mare "Lady Gray" with which he used to hunt regularly when Master of the Craven. The old mare is to be given a light job to finish up her days in peace, but when the hounds are meeting in the locality the committee are taking precautions against losing the triple mower which has only recently been installed. *Newbury Weekly News*

*

The Boy's Bogey Competition was played on Tuesday and resulted as follows: Burridge 9 down; D. Bonham Carter 11 down; P. Sandbach 13 down; J.D.R. Elkington and Arthur Pearce 15 down; Jack Hughes 16 down. *Newbury Weekly News*

1925

Caddies may not be booked more than seven days ahead. Also the member who ordered the caddie and did not turn up, shall pay for the round as if it had been played.

*

It was decided to charge the professional 7/6d a week for his cottage.

1926

Locker rents (ladies). With reference to outstanding ladies locker rents, the secretary stated that he had been informed by Mrs Urling that there was a feeling on the part of some of the lady members that they should pay 10/- for the first year's rent and 5 shillings per annum afterwards, instead of the present annual charge of 10/-.
After discussion the committee decided that in view of the fact that the ladies enjoy the same privileges as the men for 3/5ths of the male subscription they could not see their way to reduce the ladies locker rent and were of the opinion that it was rather ingratious of the ladies to cavil at the cost of the lockers. The secretary was instructed to write to Mrs Urling to this effect, with a list of the outstanding rents and a request that they be settled forthwith.

*

Hughes be instructed not to divulge results of running bogey while competition is in progress.

*

It was a matter for congratulations that Mr Hope had reached the BB&O Amateur Championship semi-final at Sonning, being put out by the ultimate winner, R.W.A. Speed.

Letter was read from Mr Brooke-Meares offering 7 or 8 head of Indian deer and bison. Secretary was instructed to notify the club's acceptance and cordial appreciation of the gift.

*

Two "holes in one" have recently been scored at the Newbury course. Mr E.T. Povey on the 5th (3rd) and Jack Steptoe on the 11th (9th). The members of the club are holding their annual dinner on May 1, and Povey has expressed his willingness to pay the penalty in the usual way on that occasion. *Newbury Weekly News*

*

A novel match recently took place between two sons of Mr Malcolm Aird. Ronald Aird, who is one of the best racquets players in the country, played round with a racquets racquet and ball, against his brother M.H. Aird, who plays ordinary golf. Through the green the former was allowed to pick up the ball and drive it with his racquet, but, once on the putting green he had to leave it on the carpet and strike it into the hole using his racquet like a billiard cue.
The players were all square at the end of the match. *Newbury Weekly News*

*

The Baxendale Cup was won by Mrs Harry Stradling (18) with a net score of 85. Mrs Harold Bance (18) had the same score, but had in error driven from the men's tee on the 14th hole.

*

"See me kill that starling" said J.B. Lee as he was about to drive off the 1st tee. Sure enough the ball hit the starling, which was about 100 yards away, killing it instantaneously. No one was more surprised than the driver. *Newbury Weekly News*

1927
Mr Brooke-Meares was thanked for several large heads which now adorn the walls of the clubhouse.

*

The Secretary be authorised to buy a meat safe.

*

It was agreed that Field be authorised to employ a woman at 6p per hour on necessary days.

*

The question of payment and cost of new winners' boards was brought up and Mr Fairhurst having announced that this might be regarded as presented by himself, a vote of thanks was moved by the chairman, which was unanimously accorded.

*

A letter was read from Colonel Stanton suggesting the introduction of tennis courts in front of the stables. Refused.

1928

It being recommended that screw on shoes be provided for the black mare. Approved.

*

Instead of taking another man for the summer try a boy at 14 shillings per week.

*

One of the competitors in the Portal Cup (Flag) J. B. Lee, whose allowance is 88 shots, reached the last green in his 86th shot, but owing to a mistake in addition on the part of his marker, and not having kept a table of his score himself, picked his ball off the green and planted his flag under the impression that he had played 88 shots. His marker, before leaving the green discovered his mistake and called Lee back, who then holed out in two more shots.

Decision: Under Rule 13 governing stroke competitions the penalty is two strokes and Mr Lee therefore takes second place.

(J. B. Lee was compensated by winning the same trophy the following year).

*

It was agreed to raise Riches from £2.10s a week to £3 a week from June 1st.

*

This was treated as an informal meeting to discuss action in connection with pilfering from the locker room. No minutes were taken.

*

The ladies April medal was won by Miss M. Platt with 100 – 15 = 85, the only return.

1929

The Secretary put forward a request from the steward that, as the bar closed at 8.30, the premises be closed at 9 pm. This is in view of the fact that his legs were beginning to break out again as they did last year.

Newbury Lady Golfers taking part in Mrs. Baxendale's Cup - 1930. Group taken in front of the Newbury District Club House with Mrs. W.K.T. Hope, the winner, holding the cup

1930
In response to a request of the Prince of Wales through Admiral Halsey it was decided
to purchase a copy of the Legion Book.

The syndicate have held a meeting and having had under consideration the present
position of the club have decided:
1.   To raise the subscription for new members to £6.6.0 for Gentlemen and £5.5.0 for
Ladies.
2.   To recommend to the general committee that
     a) A change be made in the professional and
     b) Jack Hughes be given a trial in that position
3.   The Syndicate will put forward a proposal whereby the members of the club can
     take over the arrangement, control and financial responsibilities of the club.

The membership records of Newbury District Golf Club do not go back to 1923. However, the following lists have been compiled from newspaper cuttings, competition records and minute books, covering the first five years.

The names are listed as they first appeared in the various records, but this does not indicate the actual date of their joining the club.

1923	**1924**	**1925**	**1926**
D. Baxendale	L.E. Yeomans	T. Honnor	S. Widdicombe
Colonel Stanton	F.J. Kirby	Commander Douglas	Major E.R. Portal
W.K.T. Hope	J.T. Louch	G.H. Croft	C.P. Letchford
M.O. Wells	D. Baird	H.R. Metcalf	W.H. Maynard
L.A. Ormrod	T.G. Starkey-Smith	Major Saunderson	T.B. Coulson
Commander England	Captain J. Saunderson	G.H. Gascoygne	F.G. Ball
R.A. Angier	A.R. Peart	E.J. Povey	W.H. Flint
Colonel J.A. Fairhurst	A.H. Holland	N. Mackinnon	W.H. Legge
Hon. H. Mulholland	T. Carr	J.B. Lee	J. Russell
A. Saunderson	Colonel des Voeux	A. Marshall	W.H. Flint
A.D. Pilkington	C.H. Clark	E.H. Bance	A.P. Davies
Hugh Turner	Colonel Baker	G.R. Elliott	W.H. Legge
J. Greenshields	General Comber	E.A.W. Stroud	J. Russell
L.R.J. Wasey	A. Riddock	J.E. Robson	E. Hammond
Major Tilney	A.A. Barrett	A.T. Hedden	J.P.R. Marriott
H.D. Floyd	B. Pinniger	G. Bailey	
Dr A. Finn	A.C.E. Elliott	W.H. Lester	
	G.H. Wildish	B. de Castro	
1927	Ashley Turner	Brigadier General Combe	
C.W. Bloxsom		E.P. Plenty	
J.L. Stow		A. Rummins	
Sinclair		K. Brocklehurst	
F.H. Floyd			
E. Richardson	**Ladies 1924**	**Ladies 1927**	Mrs Stokes
W. Tredinnick	Mrs Ward	Miss Platt	Mrs Stradling
H.K. Ault	Mrs Saunderson	Miss Adnams	Mrs Bance
C.H. Lloyd	Mrs Rolfe	Miss Thornsley	Mrs A.C. Elliott
C.E. Gilroy	Mrs Muirhead	Miss Plenty	Mrs Strange
Captain N.W. Tredinnick	Mrs Baxendale	Miss Pullen	
W. Smith	Mrs Cosmo Douglas	Mrs Harley	
H. Stradling	Mrs Bramwell Davis	Mrs Stow	
C.H. Godwin	Miss L. Urling	Mrs Pellows	
Gifford Wells	Miss Kitcat	Mrs Austin Dickson	
C.R. de la Salle	Mrs Baird	Mrs Borgnis	
W.S. Raine			
F.S. Constant	**Juniors – 1924 Competition**		
H.S. Tyndall	D. Bonham Carter	S. McDougall	Hughes*
H. Russell	P. Sandbach	A.C. Butler	Stroud
G.T. Belgrove	J.D.R. Elkington	I.D. Moir	Gray
	R.O.R. Clarke	Burridge	
	C. Borgnis	Pearce*	

Names with initials were members, those without were caddies.

*Arthur Pearce and Jack Hughes, still members today.

6

Pre-War Years 1931 – 1939

When the Captain's Cup, presented by Colonel Fairhurst, was played for in 1931, there was additional interest. The conditions of the competition stated that the cup would be won outright by anyone winning it for a third time. By 1931 there were three players who had won it twice, W.K.T. Hope, 1924 and 1930; N.W. Tredinnick, 1925 and 1928; and J.B. Lee, 1926 and 1929.

The leaders after one round were Admiral Coppinger (9) net 73, W.K.T. Hope (1) and Hugh Turner (13) both net 74. Tredinnick (9) was well behind on net 82. Lee was not mentioned at all. Tredinnick, out late in the afternoon scored a net 67, total 149, winning by one shot, and therefore becoming the outright winner of the Captain's Cup. Colonel Fairhurst, when making the presentation, announced that he would be pleased to present another cup. It is the replacement cup that has since then been played for as The Fairhurst Cup.

Other competition results in this period included a double by Mrs Arthur Elliott in 1933 when she won the Douglas Cup on a Monday, beating Mrs Starkey-Smith by 4 and 3, and the Platt Cup the following day, scoring 178 (32) 146 over 36 holes. The handicap limit for the Platt Cup was 24, and it was played in conjunction with a monthly medal. This was won by Miss Douglas, with an 18 hole score of 95-33-62.

In 1934 another notable double was performed when H.C. Smith, of Highclere, won the Portal Cup on Easter Sunday, and the Kirby Cup on Easter Monday.

Also in 1934 Freddie Ball, a future president, won the Ronaldshay Cup, playing off 7 handicap. Another name that appears in that year is Major Lloyd, who is remembered by the writer as a cricketer. It was thrilling to watch Major Lloyd batting for Newbury. An aggressive

Freddie Ball and his sister Margaret displaying the spoils of 1935-6

left-hander, he scored a double century in an afternoon game at Northcroft in 1948.

1935 saw the arrival of the Clifford Cup. The donor, Councillor Reggie Clifford, lived from 1918 at the Dower House in Newbury, where he ran a renowned antiques business, his distinguished clientèle including Queen Mary. He died, at the Dower House, in 1953. Clifford specified that his cup should be restricted to players of 14 handicap and above.

The report in the local paper makes interesting reading:

> It was a bogey competition and the committee had decided that it should be played under the system according to which competitors score as follows:
> 1 point for a hole done in net one over bogey
> 2 points for net bogey
> 3 points for net eagle
> 4 points for net albatross

Familiar? This is the system we now know as stableford, which was devised by Dr Frank Stableford. The new idea, was first tested at his own club, Wallasey, in May 1932. At the time of the new Clifford Cup, 1935, this points scoring system had spread through the country but was not immediately named "stableford".

Dr Stableford was captain at Wallasey in 1933, and a life member in 1953. He committed suicide at the age of 88, when after years of failing eyesight, he was told he was losing his sight altogether.

Other cups introduced in this period, were: The Boake Cup, presented by Miss R.C. Boake, 1938; The Philbrick Bowl, 1934, presented by the Misses M.E. & E.C. Philbrick; The Stokes Salver, donated by Miss M. Stokes in 1937. Mr C.E. Gilroy presented a pair of cups for mixed foursomes in 1929.

**Early Golf Equipment
at Newbury**

Members of the Committees: Miss Boake, Miss Atkinson, Mr A. Goodeve-Docker, Miss Jean Elkington, Mr C.W. Bloxsom, Mr Harold Bance and Mr Michael Barton.

This picture was taken on New Year's Eve 1937/38, at the Chequers Hotel.

> On the stroke of midnight a bearded old man (Old Tom Morris, played by Mr A. Goodeve-Docker) drove off a monster golf ball from which burst the New Year (Miss Jean Elkington) *Newbury Weekly News.*

The remainder of the report of the evening, attended by 260 people, was devoted to descriptions, in great detail, of the dresses of ten of the ladies.

> The most becoming dress in the room was of pale pink lace with a Juliet cap to match, worn with a dark blue lace redingote.

Such emphasis by the local paper must have done much for dress sales in the future, whilst grossly putting up the overall cost of attending the function.

The Baxendales and Greenham Lodge

Lloyd Harry Baxendale (born 1858 died 1937), was the son of Mr. Lloyd Baxendale who purchased Greenham Lodge estate in 1873. Educated at Eton and Christ Church, Oxford, he followed his father as a partner in the firm of Pickford & Co., of which his grandfather was a founder. Pickford and Carter Patterson & Co amalgamated in 1912 and Baxendale became chairman of the joint board of the two companies.

Lloyd H. Baxendale was a justice of the peace for Berkshire, and was chairman of the Newbury bench from 1927 to 1935, when he retired owing to deafness, being succeeded by Colonel J.A. Fairhurst.

When the Berkshire County Council was formed in 1889, Mr Baxendale was elected for the Speen Division, which included the parishes of Greenham, Enborne and Hamstead Marshall.

He had a great deal to do with the formation of Newbury Racecourse, which was laid out, and the grandstands erected, on land which was part of the Greenham Lodge Estate. Mr Baxendale was a close friend of the famous Newbury trainer, John Porter. They played an annual cricket match, each being captain of his side, and on one occasion Tom Emmett and the Australian Spofforth, "the demon bowler", appeared, one on each side.

It was Porter who in 1903 suggested the suitability of the present racecourse site to Mr Baxendale, who immediately recognised the possibilities and gave Porter an option on the land required. As with the golf club, Mr Baxendale served on a "promoting syndicate" as chairman when the company was formed.

When King George V and Queen Mary visited the racecourse, they were always received by Mr Baxendale, and the royal box was decorated by Charles Dalby, head gardener at Greenham Lodge.

For many years Baxendale ran a cricket week on his excellent cricket ground, which in recent years has been a baseball field for the residents of Greenham Common Airbase, between the 15th hole and the Lodge. The ground was prepared by Dalby, and many famous cricketers appeared there.

In Baxendale's obituary in 1937 the following emotive paragraph appeared:

> He loved Greenham Common. Some people might have had the idea that he carried out his duties of Lord of the Manor too strictly, but it was to him that the amenities of the common were strictly observed and its picturesqueness preserved. He handed down a glorious tract of country, which under the Law of Property Act will be secured for all time to the public, for their rest and recreation. *Newbury Weekly News*

How sad he would have been, had he survived a few more years, to see his beloved common confiscated and mostly converted into an airbase of international notoriety.

How much sadder would he be now, with the airbase redundant, to witness the reluctance to return it to the public.

When the Greenham Lodge estate was auctioned in 1938, following the death of Lloyd H. Baxendale, there was considerable anxiety, not only for the future of the common, but for the future of the golf course. Should the estate have fallen into the hands of speculators, then the imminent expiry of the lease could have been the end of golf at Greenham.

To the rescue came Captain Guy Baxendale, who bought, for £14,000, Greenham Lodge, the golf course, and Pigeons Farm. Captain Baxendale was a nephew of Lloyd H. Baxendale, and grandson of the late Mr Baxendale, senior. It was his concern that the family ties with the Lodge and estate would be severed that prompted him to make the purchase and, subsequently, sell his house in Sussex and return to Greenham Lodge, where he was born.

Captain Guy Baxendale

Also being auctioned was the Lordship of the Manor. Some members of the Newbury Corporation secretly decided to attempt to buy the title for the benefit of the community. They did not put the matter to the council until a

Lloyd H.Baxendale, centre, tallest figure with buttonhole, with King George V and Queen Mary at Newbury Races 1933

finance committee meeting held the day after the purchase had taken place.

The title was sold for £225 and it was generally acknowledged that bidding was deliberately withheld, and Councillor Frank Shergold, acting for the corporation, was the only bidder.

There was a general relief that there was now a certain future for the common and the commoners: "Safeguarding the amenities of the common and ensuring that members of the public have right of access to it for air and exercise".

These pleasures were to last for little more than one year.

Then fences appeared, and tarmac covered the heather – and all was lost.

Apart from necessary obligations during the Second World War, Newbury Golf Club finally lost none of its course but now, in 1994, the fences still contain all of the "common land" within the obsolete air base.

The Lordship of the Manor, to this day, has proved of little value, when all decisions are imposed by the Ministry of Defence, who seem reluctant to recognise obligations.

Short Game

1931

A recommendation to the captain, signed by 29 members, urging the "retention for a trial period of Jack Hughes as professional when the post becomes vacant".

In view of the strong feeling amongst members (many more signatures could have been obtained) in favour of giving Hughes a trial it was decided that Hughes be given a trial for six months as professional from April 1st or whenever the post becomes vacant at a weekly salary of 30/-, to be confirmed by the syndicate.

The secretary to inform Hughes accordingly and to ask Hughes to inform him if in the meantime he should be stood off by Riches.

*

Mr Hope's application to play in the native English Amateur Championship was endorsed by the club.

*

Mr Gilroy proposed Mr W.K.T. Hope as captain, remarking that he was the best golfer in the club, and was very popular amongst all the members. (Applause)

1932

Mr Cowper praised Whitlock for his oversight of the course.

*

The original hole tins had been replaced by Pattison's anti-mud hole tins which prevent the pins from damaging the edges of the holes.

*

The hay which had been made will further reduce the bill for horsekeep.

The purchase of a bull terrier for the protection of the club premises was approved. The steward to bear half the cost.

1933
Cyril Tolley and Roger Wethered (Tadley) are to play at Newbury.

1934
It was agreed to light the club with Aladdin lamps to be purchased from Hickman & Metcalf.

1935
Overhanging lips to all bunkers to be increased.

*

Mr Widdicombe generously offered to put up the Urling Bowl, which he won some years ago. (Monthly Bogey Qualifying)

*

The committee recommended to the syndicate that the horse be dispensed with.

1936
It was agreed that Hughes should be paid 10/- each time he plays in a club match.

*

Hughes was given permission to play at Hoylake. (Open Championship)
Jack Hughes, playing with W.S. Paine went round in 66. Not being satisfied with that, he went out in the evening with C. de V Buckingham, and returned a 63, which included a six at the 9th (7th) where he went out of bounds with his second shot.

*

It was agreed that the present sucker rule should be altered to include all suckers.

*

Thanks were expressed to Admiral Moir for the loan of the picture of "Old Tom". (Admiral Moir was the grandson of the founder of Crookham, Captain R. Dashwood Fowler. He died at sea during the war. His body was never recovered).

1937
Hughes retaining fee was considered and it was decided to ask him to submit a statement of his income.

1938
The prize for Captain's Day was given for the best 36 hole eclectic score, won by John Widdicombe (14) net 58, second F.B. Barton (8) net 59, third K. Huxtable (18) net 59.

*

The final of the Paul Jones foursomes was played on Wednesday. (The winners at the end of each round drawing afresh for partners and opponents).

A letter was received from Mr Elliott regarding a male representative on the ladies committee, and the Secretary was requested to enquire what had happened to Major Tilney!

*

Hole-in-One. It was agreed to abandon the observance of the ancient ritual in connection with the performance of this feat.

1939

Chicken manure. Resolved to order 2 loads at 5/- a load and compare by testing on the same green as pig manure, but advisable to use sparingly.

Slade's manure is good if selected.

It was resolved that 30 yards of pig manure be ordered.

*

A scheme proposed by Highclere Golf Club that Newbury and Highclere members share each other courses, with no extra charges for the duration of the war, was rejected.

7

Wartime and After 1939 – 1946

The tragedies of war were more immediately apparent in 1939 than they had been in 1918, when headlines and articles covered the war, but there was no news photograph, and even the worst news was somehow subdued in the small print.

From 1939 the local paper included many photographs of young men who had died, or were missing, and sport was immediately reduced to triviality.

In July 1940 there appeared a headline "Great golf in final of Ronaldshay Cup", and a sub heading "F.N. Ball wins for fourth time." In the adjacent columns were photographs of very young men: Sapper A.F. Rivers, missing believed dead; Hermitage cricketers, Pte E. Burgess and Pte A. Buckle, missing; Pte F.W. Cottrill, missing believed dead. At the foot of the column was an appeal under the heading "Information Wanted", a plea from the parents of Pte Albert Willis, posted as missing, last heard of in a casualty clearing station with gun shot head injuries. There were many more such appeals on the same page.

Although it was desirable that life should appear as normal as possible, the golf club sensitively abandoned all competitions, although some were restored a few months later.

In the minutes of a committee meeting held on September 17th 1939, under the sub-title "War time policy", it was emphatically resolved that the club would carry on during the war. The next notes referred to their anticipation, and fear, that they may be required to "plough up the land", and Mr Hagger was appointed to argue their case, should this occur.

At the same meeting it was decided that temporary membership was to be offered to members of the services, for a fee of one shilling per day.

In December 1939, 14 months after Mr Guy Baxendale purchased the golf course, he wrote to the club as follows:

Dear Sir,

I am wondering whether the Newbury District Golf Club would care to consider my extending the present lease from its expiring date in 1943 to 1950, but paying an increase in rent of £60 per annum. Perhaps you will in due course let me hear.

Yours faithfully,

Guy Baxendale.

A reply was drafted by Mr S. Widdicombe, submitted to the Syndicate for their approval and subsequently sent to Mr Baxendale.

22nd January 1940
Dear Sir,
Your letter of the 26th December has been considered by the members of the Syndicate and by the General Purposes Committee of the Newbury District Golf Club, who have requested me to give you the following information on the question of the renewal of the Club's lease:

After its establishment in 1922 the annual accounts of the Club showed almost every year a financial loss and this has been the case until the past 2 or 3 years when owing to the action of Colonel Fairhurst – who most generously announced his intention to forego the loan and accumulated interest due to him amounting to upwards of £3,200 – the Club has been able to show a small profit during 3 out of the past 4 years. The outbreak of war has, of course, seriously affected the financial position of the Club and, notwithstanding the economies which are being effected wherever possible, it is practically certain that during the present year and in future years during which the war may continue substantial losses will be incurred in the running of the Club.

The members of the Committee therefore find great difficulty in dealing with your suggestion that in consideration of an extension of the lease an increased rent should be payable as from the commencement of the next quarter. This suggestion is one which would have to be placed before a General Meeting of the members, where it would inevitably obtain general publicity in the town and district, and it is felt that this should be avoided if possible.

The Committee are advised that the fair annual value of the lands comprising the Golf Course, if used for agricultural purposes, would be less than half of the rent now being paid and they feel that the present rent must be regarded as a high one, particularly having regard to the liabilities of the lessees as laid down in the present lease.

The Committee are of the opinion that any extension should be for a further period of not less than 21 years and they consider that the annual rent during the new period should not be more than the present rent of £200 per annum.

The members of the Syndicate and Committee would however be glad if you would agree to meet representatives of the Club when next you are in the district, for the purpose of discussing the whole matter, as there are several points which require detailed explanation and discussion, and the representatives of the Club would appreciate the opportunity of expressing their views to you personally.
Yours faithfully,
C.W. Bloxsom.
Honorary Secretary

Captain Baxendale replied in March, 1940 his letter ending

"....As regards your letter of 22nd Jan. I am not prepared to consider your suggestion, and mine having been declined, matters had best rest where they are".

As predicted, on May 22nd 1941, a requisition was received from the Ministry of Defence, which resulted in the loss, for the duration of the war, and a little beyond, of most of the golf course. Courses, particularly links on the east coast, were especially vulnerable to the needs of war, being more easily converted to airfields. Newbury was lucky to retain at least some holes.

As can be seen in the illustration, the air base, as built for the war (much smaller than that later constructed for the Cold War) had concrete and tarmac taxiways built across the 1st, 14th and 15th fairways.

In any good summer a diagonal strip becomes evident across the 1st fairway, stretching from the bunkers to the green. There are changes in the quality and colour of the turf, clearly showing the path of "taxiway 14".

At the same time, the outline of a wartime hut appears alongside the 14th green, hauntingly reminding us of the past.

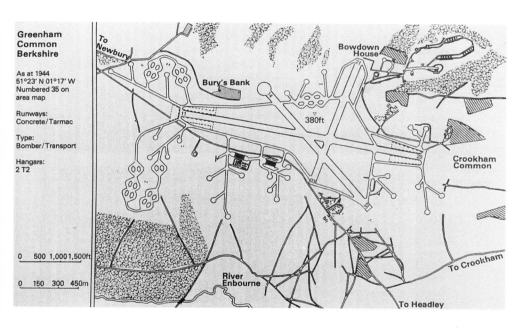

The 14th hole was devastated from tee to green, as described by Frank Barton in a later chapter. Forty years later when the men's 15th tee was moved to its present position, a 100 yard path of concrete, which stretched in front of the new tee, had to be removed.

Meanwhile, the lower holes were confiscated for the grazing of sheep and cattle, taking out the present 4th, 5th, 6th, 7th, 8th and 9th. A fence was erected between these holes and the remainder of the course.

The "course" played throughout the war consisted of only seven holes: 1st tee to present 10th green; 11, 12 and 13 were played as now; 14th tee to 16th green; 17th and 18th remained as usual.

NEWBURY & DISTRICT GOLF CLUB

Greenham Common,
NEWBURY.

20th April, 1942.

Dear Sir or Madam,

I have been asked by the Club Committee to write to each member in reference to the crisis with which the Club is now faced owing to the war and especially to the new regulations affecting the use of petrol likely to come into force in June next.

The situation is that since the commencement of the war the revenue of the Club has been steadily diminishing and that unless (1) the present revenue is at least maintained and (2) a substantial reduction of the expenditure can be effected, it will not be possible to avoid the closing down of the Club and the course. If this happens it is almost certain that the course could not be re-opened after the war. The Committee feel therefore that the closing of the course should be avoided if at all possible, as they believe that the great majority of the members will wish to know that after the war they will have the opportunity of playing on the course again.

The present lease of the property comprising the course and the buildings expires in September, 1943, and the Committee, who have been in negotiation with Capt. Guy Baxendale (the owner of the property) for some time past, have been advised by him that he would be prepared to grant a further lease on reasonable terms to trustees nominated by and acting on behalf of the members of the Club.

The Committee have gone very carefully into the question of reducing the cost of upkeep and have decided that temporarily the top nine holes only shall be kept in play and that a minimum of work shall be done on the remainder of the course. By this means it is estimated that a saving of about £200 per annum will be made. It is, however, essential that every member, whether able to play on the course or not, should do all within his power to maintain the Club in existence. I am therefore, by the wish of the Committee, submitting to every member the form printed on the back hereof asking the member to state the extent to which he or she is prepared to help at this critical time. I feel confident that the members will rally around the Club to the utmost of their ability, and I am taking it upon myself to make the following suggestions :—

    1.   To those on service or otherwise compelled to live away from the district :
         Undertake to pay at least one-half of the normal subscription and promise more if possible.

    2.   To those who can play on the course infrequently :
         Continue the subscription at the normal rate and if possible assist with a donation to improve the present unsatisfactory cash position.

    3.   To those who can play fairly regularly :
         Continue the annual subscription and give an additional sum until the war is over.

    4.   There may be some non-playing members who may be able to increase their annual subscription or make a donation to help the present financial position.

I am enclosing a stamped addressed label and ask you to be good enough to send me your reply on the form by return, if possible, but in any case not later than the 30th April, as the Committee will meet immediately after that date and their report and recommendations will be submitted to a general meeting of the members to be held *at the Club* on Saturday, the 9th May, at 2.30 p.m. I have been asked to make it clear that this letter is intended to be a notice of that meeting and to express the hope that every member who can will make a special point of being present. There will be a good deal of business to be transacted at the meeting, including the appointment of a new Honorary Secretary in the place of Mr. Bloxsom, who has been obliged to resign the appointment after holding it for 16 years. Any suggestions from the members to promote the interest of the Club, which will be welcomed by the Committee, should be attached to the form.

If the meeting of members is to be in a position to decide whether the Club shall be carried on, it is essential that every member shall make a point of replying to this letter by the date mentioned, April 30th next. If sufficient promises of support are not received, the Committee will have no option but to recommend the meeting to close down the Club.

Yours faithfully

3 May 1942.   Chairman   J. A. Fairhurst.

                                             [P.T.O.

The minute books of those days reflect no discontent, rarely reporting anything other than what appeared to be normal club affairs.

The first taste of war came at midday on December 15th 1941 when a Miles Master Mk1 aircraft, from the Operational Training Unit, crashed close to Greenham Lodge, damaging the 15th fairway. The 15th was then a par 4 and was closer to the Lodge than it is today.

The pilot, Sgt S.P. Kurek, RCAF, and the passenger, AC1 I. Hackett, RAFVR, were killed instantly.

Due to wartime security there was no report, or pictures in the newspapers. The event only came to light when Mr Charles Smith, of Thatcham, who had responded to an advertisement, for memories and photographs of Crookham Golf Club, recalled watching the aircraft crash. Subsequently the Ministry of Defence confirmed the incident. The club minutes for January 4th 1942 read:

> The Secretary read a letter from the Damage Officer, No 50 MU RAF Cowley, Oxford, regretting the damage done to the 15th fairway when a Miles Master training plane crashed on the course on the 15th December and expressing the hope that in view of the small amount of damage caused the Committee might waive their right to claim compensation.
>
> The Committee came to the conclusion that in view of the critical situation of the clubs finances they felt bound to claim the actual cost of repairing the damage which is estimated at £3.

In the period 1942-46, there were more critical decisions and major changes made than in the entire history of the Newbury District Club and the subsequent Newbury & Crookham Club. The 1942 annual general meeting was certainly not one to be missed.

The letter from Colonel Fairhurst circulated to the members had, in its final paragraph, expressed pessimism regarding the future of the club. The response had been excellent and the treasurer reported that the club would remain solvent as a result of the promises made. Sir Leonard Lyle dramatically proposed that the club should carry on!

The committee was able to announce that Captain Guy Baxendale had agreed to renew the lease on the expiry of the present lease in 1943.

The Syndicate chose this time to announce that they were prepared to transfer their rights and responsibilities to the club members at an appropriate time. The Syndicate, particularly Colonel Fairhurst, were praised for the way they had nursed the club through its first 20 years. Trustees were appointed to replace the Syndicate: Hugh Turner, E. Harold Bance, W.K.T. Hope and S. Widdicombe.

The resignation of the Syndicate officially occurred in 1943.

Since the club had opened in 1923, lady members enjoyed no status in the management of the club, but in the future they would be represented on the new committee by their captain and secretary.

The honorary secretary Mr C.W. Bloxsom, who had held the post since 1926, announced his retirement. Mr L.E. Yeomans was elected to replace him. Mr Bloxsom was elected an honorary life member of the club.

Having been president since the inauguration of the club, the Marquis of Zetland (previously the Earl of Ronaldshay) expressed his intention to step down and proposed that Colonel Fairhurst should succeed him. This was unanimously approved.

C. W. Bloxsom

Colonel James Ashton Fairhurst, TD, DL, JP, MA. (1868 – 1944)

Colonel Fairhurst was born in Wigan, the son of a brewer. Educated at Rugby and Jesus College, Cambridge, he became a barrister of the Inner Temple. He was a major and hon. lieut. colonel of the 5th Manchester Regiment, and was awarded the Territorial Decoration.

Colonel Fairhurst maintained his interest in the brewery until his father's death in 1912. He married the eldest daughter of William Ansell of Wylde Green, Warwickshire, the proprietor of the well known Ansell's brewery of Birmingham, of which he later became chairman of the directors.

Colonel Fairhurst moved to Arlington Manor (now Mary Hare Grammar School) in 1905. By 1908 he had become joint master of the Craven Hounds, which post he held until 1921, being the master for the last two years. Apart from being a pioneer of the golf club, Colonel Fairhurst was largely responsible for the formation of Newbury Rugby Club in 1926, and, upon the death of Lloyd H. Baxendale in 1938, he became chairman of the Newbury Racecourse Co. Ltd.

The colonel played golf until 1937, by which time he was finding the hills too much for him. He continued to serve, and subsidise, the golf club in the years following, seldom missing a meeting of general or sub-committees.

Colonel Fairhurst presided over several war-effort committees, was a governor of St Bartholomew's Grammar School, was a JP, and a supporter of many local organisations.

TO:-

The Secretary, Committee and Members,

Newbury District Golf Club,

Greenham,

NEWBURY.

I, JAMES ASHTON FAIRHURST of Arlington Manor near Newbury
in the County of Berks Esquire do by this deed declare as
follows:-

WHEREAS at various times I have for good and sufficient
reasons paid on behalf of the above-named Club various sums
for improvements and other matters which with interest thereon
at Five per centum from the dates of payment by me are now
represented in the last Balance Sheet of the said Club dated
the Thirty first day of May One thousand nine hundred and
thirty six by the sum of Three thousand two hundred pounds and
I am now desirous of releasing and discharging the Committee
Officers and Members from all liability with regard to the said
debt as from such last mentioned date.-

NOW THIS DEED WITNESSETH that in pursuance of my said
desire I hereby absolutely release and discharge the Committee
Officers and Members of the said Club from all or any liability
present or future with regard to the said debt and from all
accounts claims and demands whatsoever in respect thereof.-

AS WITNESS my hand and seals this   *Fifth*   day of July
One thousand nine hundred and thirty seven.

SIGNED SEALED and DELIVERED by)

the said James Ashton Fairhurst)

in the presence of:-   )   *J. a. Fairhurst.*

John Couch

Solicitor

Newbury

There is no doubt that Colonel Fairhurst has been the most influential person in the history of golf in Newbury. Although he died before the Newbury and Crookham clubs united, he influenced golf far beyond the date of his death in 1944, simply because there would have been no golf course but for him. It was his idea, was built through his efforts, and mostly financed by his money. He was its guardian and father figure for 21 years and saw a satisfactory result of his efforts when – only four months before his death – his syndicate felt that the club had matured sufficiently to be trusted to conduct its own affairs. He did not live to see the purchase of the course in 1946, or the merger of the two clubs, but it is most likely that he had already anticipated these possibilities.

The Merger

The Newbury District Golf Club had much to contend with in the early 1940s, as had many golf clubs throughout the country. Apart from there being a shortage of golfers, there was little remaining of their course. They dealt with the battles over compensation, uncertainty over the future, the mammoth task of removing a runway, and the transferring of power from the founding Syndicate to the membership.

Those who represented the club's interest throughout this period showed superb resilience but, above all, a remarkable generosity in their attitude and gestures towards Crookham Golf Club.

Imagine the despair of the Crookham members, having almost their whole course requisitioned and seeing their new clubrooms, built only four years earlier adjoining the Volunteer Inn, razed to the ground.

Their despair was obviously laced with a dogged optimism, if not realism, and their committee continued to bind the membership together, negotiating with the Newbury Club for a "temporary arrangement" for Crookham members to play at Newbury. This hospitality lasted from 1940 until 1945 when, at the Newbury District AGM, the first sign of a permanent solution was minuted:

> Mr Widdicombe welcomed the members from Crookham Golf Club and thanked them for their support. A question asked as to the position of the Crookham members in the future, was left to the committee to settle as soon as possible.

The immediate result of this renewed interest was that Crookham members were offered equal rights with Newbury members if they were willing to pay the same subs, and this was accepted by the still active Crookham committee in March 1946. However, it was when the letter of acceptance of this offer was read out in the March 1946 general committee meeting, that Mr de Vere Buckingham proposed that the two clubs should combine entirely under the name of Newbury & Crookham Golf Club.

This proposal was carried at a special general meeting, involving both clubs on April 24th 1946.

The generosity referred to may have been a phenomenon of the effect of war, for it is hard to imagine such a gesture being repeated today.

Crookham, by 1946, had nothing left but memories. It had no money, no course, no equipment, and virtually no members – perhaps 20 in total.

What it did have, however, were its priceless, historic cups, the two dating from 1874 being two of the oldest in golf (now the Newbury & Crookham Bogey and Newbury & Crookham Medal).

This sequence of events perpetuated the name of Crookham and brought credit to the Newbury District Club. Together as Newbury & Crookham Golf Club, they moved into a new era, which has to this day been free of any of the turmoil, tension and uncertainty of the years preceding.

The Newbury District committee throughout the period covering the amalgamation of the two clubs was:

Jack Whiting and Jack Hughes travelled together to Reading 1939 to enlist, but chose separate forces, Hughes going for the Army, but Whiting preferring the RAF. Hughes recalls this fact with some envy, for Whiting immediately found himself stationed with Henry Cotton, and being a high quality golfer, was directed to play several exhibition games with Cotton. Cotton and Whiting are (left to right) in the centre.

President: A.S.B. Tull; captain: E.T. Povey; hon. sec: P.H. Greader; hon. treasurer: R. Kerr and Messrs E.H. Bance, C de V. Buckingham, R.M Codd, W.K.T. Hope, S. Widdicombe and M. Barton (Michael Barton was the last survivor).

W.K.T. Hope served on the committee throughout the entire life of the club prior to the amalgamation, being captain in 1931-1933 and always its strongest player.

Mr C. de Vere Buckingham on the practice ground with the 13th fairway in the background

Short Game

1940

Discussion took place over a letter from the War Agricultural Committee regarding grazing sheep on the course. Mr Wilson pointed out that a maximum of 200 sheep would in two months eat the rough down and have a very poor living owing to the poor quality of the rough, and the sheep would probably go back in condition.

*

Camp Hopson & Co. be asked to submit estimates for black-out efficient where necessary on the club premises.

*

The committee discussed suggestions that women engaged in Red Cross and similar duties should be permitted to pay a reduced green fee and decided that the reduced fee be applicable only to the ATS.

1941

As a result of the inspection by the War Agricultural Executive Committee, no ploughing of the course would be required but sheep would have to be put on for a period.

*

It was reported that the Air Ministry would probably take over part of the course.

*

Mr Bance reported a satisfactory result of his negotiations with representatives of the Air Ministry by which further acquisition of land would not affect the 13th hole and would permit use of the 1st hole.

*

It was suggested that members of the Crookham Golf Club should be allowed to play on the course after 5pm each day at a reduced green fee of 1/6d.
(First mention of Crookham Golf Club in any minutes of Newbury District Golf Club).

*

The secretary was instructed to write to Mr de Castro conveying to him grateful thanks and also to Mr Ben Warner for his great assistance in keeping the 19th playable.

*

The Committee confirmed the action taken with regard to Whitlock whose wages had been raised to £4.7.6 per week. The secretary was instructed to write expressing appreciation for his services and assuring him that after the war his steadfast devotion to the club would not be forgotten.

*

As the Crookham Club had ceased to function for the time being it was decided that the membership fee for bona fide members of the Crookham Golf Club be £3.3.0 for the duration, or for those not joining, 2/- per round.

1943

Mr Wallis was willing to continue to graze the lower holes.

It was expected that at least 12 members of the Crookham Golf Club would become members.

*

Arrangements had been made for a shepherd to work on the course for $2^1/_2$ days each week for a weekly payment of 15/- extra.

*

A claim was being made to the Air Ministry for compensation with respect to the injury sustained by the club in consequence of the requisitioning of parts of the golf course.

*

It was agreed to pay the funeral expenses of the late steward and also pay to Mrs Reeves a part of the cost of the bath installed by them.

1944

The members stood in silence in tribute to the memory of their late president, Colonel Fairhurst, and former captain, Mr C. E. Gilroy.

*

A suggestion that ladies be admitted to the bar on Saturdays and Sundays was adopted.

1945

Members stood in silence for a few moments in honour of the members who had been lost during the war. Amongst the seniors was Admiral Moir and amongst the younger members David Thomas, two of our best players.

*

The Air Ministry had agreed to de-requisition immediately the land which was taken from the club and formed part of the fairway and green of the 1st hole. With the opening up of the bottom holes, this will make 16 holes in play by the summer of 1946.

*

To try to speed up the installation of the electricity in the club premises, a petition to be written to the Wessex Electricity Company, signed by all owners and tenants in the district.

*

Proposed and seconded that Messrs Povey, Buckingham and Greader (secretary) interview Jack Hughes to explain the club's proposals to him.
It was suggested that he be paid £2 per week for work on the course in the mornings. Afternoons to be free for him to give lessons and do repairs.

1946

It was reported that Jack Hughes was prepared to accept the retaining fee of £2.10.0 (less insurances) but not the £2 per week to work on the course. This was agreed.

*

A letter from the Wessex Electricity Company stated that if the club are prepared to guarantee a minimum payment of £30 per annum for a period of five years, electricity can be supplied to the club premises.

Crookham 1878 - watercolour by Major F.P.Hopkins

Scenes from a 1968 exhibition match in which Jack Hughes partnered Neil Coles against Harry Weetman and Max Faulkner. Club captain Peter Boynton was referee

Top. Max Faulkner conducting his "Golf Clinic"

Bottom. Coles playing from the bunker on the present 2nd, watched by Weetman. The three caddies on view were Phil Risby, John Dyson and Rex Hepburn

1st hole

5th hole

6th hole

7th hole

8th hole

9th green and 10th tee

13th hole

15th hole

16th hole

9th hole

The Captains, 1995

Part III

Newbury & Crookham Golf Club

Len Moore and Jack Hughes

8

The Amalgamation

**Special General Meeting of Newbury Golf Club and Crookham Golf Club.
Held at the Newbury Clubhouse on Wednesday April 24th 1946**

Present: **Mr A.S.B. Tull (president) in the chair, supported by the full
committee of the Newbury Club.
A large attendance of Newbury and Crookham members were
present.**

Amalgamation of Newbury and Crookham Golf Clubs

Mr Widdicombe gave a review of the two clubs and then explained the
suggestion for the amalgamation of the two clubs, as follows:

> "That Crookham members be invited to join Newbury Golf Club on a full
> membership basis, at £5.5.0 for Gentlemen, and £4.4.0 for Ladies, subject to the
> response being sufficient".

This was formerly proposed by Mr Steptoe and seconded by Mr Whiting that
Crookham should join the Newbury Club at the proposed subscription. This
was carried unanimously by all the Crookham Members present.
Mr Hugh Turner proposed the amalgamation of the two clubs under the
title of The Newbury & Crookham Golf Club, this was seconded by Mr J.
Hill. This was carried unanimously.[1]

General Meetings

It was decided that both clubs should hold General Meetings to confirm the
proposed amalgamation under the terms suggested as soon as possible.

---

[1] This followed the original proposal by Mr D. de V. Buckingham at an earlier Newbury
District committee meeting.

The 1946 Exhibition Match

The match was arranged to commemorate the marriage of the Newbury and Crookham clubs.

Lord Lyle (of Tate & Lyle Ltd) was a member and was able to induce Reg Whitcombe, the Parkstone professional to play. Whitcombe, one of four famous professional brothers, won the Open Championship in the howling gales at Sandwich in 1938. He was an English International and Ryder Cup player (1935).

Jack Hughes driving in the 1946 Exhibition Match

Standing; M.Barton, S.Dell, W.K.T.Hope, R.Whitcombe, J.R.Beck, J.Hughes, H.Bramley Davenport, S.Widdicombe, H.Bance, C. de Vere Buckingham

Seated: E.Povey, A.S.B.Tull, Lord Lyle, P.Greader, R.M.Codd

In 1946 an exhibition match was arranged to commemorate the marriage of the Newbury and Crookham clubs.

Two leading amateurs, J.B.Beck, Walker Cup captain in 1938, and H.Bramley Davenport with Jack Hughes, made up the fourball spectacle. Beck was off plus one handicap, and Bramley Davenport off scratch. Both were made honorary members for their efforts.

Crookham Cups

Four cups having been received from the Crookham Golf Club, it was decided to play for them as follows:

The J. H. Taylor and A. S. B. Tull Cups to be challenge cups for the Mens Foursomes.

Crookham Handicap Cup to be an 18 hole Bogey Competition played in the Autumn.

Crookham Challenge Cup to be an 18 hole Medal Competition, played in the Spring.

Three Ladies Cups received from Crookham Golf Club were handed on to the Ladies to arrange their disposal: Jean Cup, Simmonds Cup, Bramwell-Davis Cup.

Throughout the late 1940s the committee was pre-occupied with reclaiming the course, from the concrete on the top holes, and mud and devastation on the lower holes. Even with patience and hard work, the course was only fully operational, with necessary adjustments, by 1951.

Imagine the shock when, in January 1951, a letter was received from the Air Ministry stating that the airfield on Greenham Common was to be taken over again, and that some part of the golf course might be required!

Fortunately this did not prove necessary and the course remained intact, although within a few months its surroundings changed dramatically with the coming of the United States Air Force, peace campers, and a different variety of bunkers.

Discussions began in 1951 between the golf club and Captain Guy Baxendale regarding the purchase of the course, and a special general meeting was called, in March 1952.

URGENT AND IMPORTANT

NEWBURY & CROOKHAM GOLF CLUB

Greenham Common,
Newbury,
14th March 1952

DEAR SIR OR MADAM,

A Special General Meeting of the members of the Club will be held in the Council Chamber at the Municipal Buildings, Newbury, on Friday, 21st March 1952, at 7.30 p.m. to consider the appended report of the Club Committee and to pass resolutions thereon.

It will be seen that the report embodies proposals of vital importance to the Club and it is earnestly hoped that every member of the Club will do his utmost to be present at the meeting as the decisions made at this meeting (and the second meeting to follow) will undoubtedly determine the future destiny of the Club.

Yours faithfully,

A.S.B. TULL, *President*

H. INMAN TAYLOR, *Captain*

P.H. GREADER, *Secretary*

REPORT OF CLUB COMMITTEE

For many months past, negotiations with Captain Guy Baxendale (which will be explained to the meeting in detail) for a long lease of the Golf Club property have been in progress.

The rent which Captain Baxendale was insisting on was such that the Club could not possibly afford to pay and ultimately proposals were made which have resulted in terms and conditions being agreed (subject to confirmation by the Club members and the settlement of minor details) for the purchase by the Club from Captain Baxendale of the freehold of the Golf Course comprising the Course, the Club buildings, the Steward's cottage and another cottage adjoining, and a plot of land on the south side of the 14th hole for the sum of £6,500. It is estimated that a total sum of £7,000 will be necessary to cover the cost of the purchase and the formation of a company as mentioned later.

The Committee have given careful consideration to various methods of raising the capital required and after making numerous enquiries, are unanimously of the opinion that the only practicable method of financing the scheme will be the formation of a company limited by Guarantee and not having a Share Capital with Articles of Association which will enable the Club to issue Debentures in multiples of £25 each to members of the Club. Such Debentures will carry no interest whilst the holder is a member of the Club, but each Debenture of £25 will entitle the member holder to a reduction of 10/6 in his or her annual subscription, so that for example a member holding four £25 Debentures would be entitled to a reduction of £2 2s. 0d. in his or her subscription. This scheme, based on a scheme which is being successfully operated by another Golf Club, has obvious advantages as it will be appreciated that if the total amount of £7,000 is raised by the taking up of Debentures in this way the total loss in subscriptions to the Club will only be £147 per annum. To this sum must be added the liability for Schedule "A" Tax for which the Club as the owner of the property will be liable, but even these two sums together do not approach our present rental, let alone the rent which Captain Baxendale would require if he granted a long lease to the Club. The scheme is also advantageous so far as members are concerned, as members at present pay their subscriptions out of their taxed income and a reduction of £2 2s. 0d. for every £100 worth of Debentures held is equivalent at the present rate of taxation to an investment of £100 bearing interest at 4%.

Too much emphasis cannot be laid upon the undoubted fact that failure of the present project would in all probability mean the beginning of the end of the Golf Club, whereas its success would lead to the establishment of the Club on a sound basis with every prospect of improvement and success in the future. Members will appreciate that the Course is only held on a yearly tenancy and the Club has no security of tenure. For this reason it will be obvious that it is essential to raise the required sum of £7,000, and every member must do his or her utmost to support the scheme.

This was a successful meeting to some extent, but the subsequent tally was only £4,800, promised by 74 members. A "Final Appeal" was sent out in April, which brought the total to £6,350, still £650 short of target. Mr K. Huxtable promised a further £300, which put the committee in a position to go back to the members, in August 1952, when all resolutions were passed, and before the end of the year the club had become Newbury & Crookham Golf Club Limited, and owned the golf course and premises.

Those of us who encounter members from other golf clubs throughout our travels, often feel relief that we are part of a "members club", free to govern our own affairs and to make our own rules and decisions. Although there are many new golf courses being constructed these days, few afford members such rights.

We should therefore be grateful to those who acted so wisely in 1952: Mr Kerr the hon. treasurer, who perhaps through fatigue, resigned at the AGM, and was made an honorary member. Freddie Ball handled all legal affairs, including the issuing of debentures. Philip Greader must have been overworked as secretary, and others closely connected with the project were: Sam Widdicombe, Frank Shergold, K. Huxtable and H. Inman Taylor. The leading debenture holders were: Mr and Mrs N.S. Bostock, 30, Mr and Mrs K. Huxtable, 28, C.M. Longden, 16, F.L. Shergold, 16, A.S.B. Tull, 10, E.H. Bance, 8, A.J. Swanson, 8.

The Dunn Trophy

For the first time, a prize was awarded for the best scratch score in the Fairhurst Cup competition in 1949, and was won by Mr John Casserley, who is currently, in 1995, a playing member of Tadmarton Heath Golf Club. Casserley is recorded as being the first winner of the Dunn Trophy, but this is technically incorrect, as that trophy was not donated until after George Dunn died in 1950. However, he was the first club "champion".

George Dunn arrived in Newbury in 1944 moving from Fraserburg, Aberdeenshire, to live with his son, and daughter-in-law. He was then 75 years old, and was delighted to find his new home was almost on the Newbury course (being the white house now occupied by Mr and Mrs John

John Casserley, first club champion (1949) watching Michael Barton driving from the present 2nd tee in the early fifties

Gilbert, alongside the 14th fairway). He immediately became attached and devoted to the golf club, as its members did to him. Clearly a popular man, he was made an honorary member of the Fraserburg Golf Club before he left, having won many trophies there, including their two oldest, the James Thomson Cup, as its first winner in 1906, and the Maconochie Cup, which he won in 1907.

Born in 1869, Dunn was golfing before the turn of the century, and was proud to recall that he had often played golf in a red coat, as was the custom in early days.

George often helped Jack in the pro shop and played regularly until only a few days before his death. He was buried in Fraserburg. His family later presented his putter to the club, which was mounted and used thereafter as the trophy for the scratch championship, each winner's golf ball being engraved and suspended from the trophy.

Possibly because the winners were unable to take the trophy home, another trophy was donated by Mr Joe Cznadel, a pre-war professional, one of the group of American airmen who played at the club from 1952. This was respectfully called the Dunn Trophy, but, surprisingly, the original trophy, club and balls, was discarded.

Fortunately, Jack Hughes spotted the club in the dustbin, rescued it, and was its custodian for the next 40 years. The club has recently (1993) been restored and golf balls engraved to bring it up to date.

From 1949 the club championship was won for the best gross score in the Fairhurst Cup. It was in 1965 that the Dunn Trophy was first played for in separate competition.

The 1950s

The Rutherford Cup of 1952 had a dramatic climax when F.N. Ball (5) and R.A. Bance (8) tied on 38 points, and were equal on the last nine, six and three holes.

On the 18th tee Bob Bance had 34 points, and he then scored an excellent four, for 4 points (the hole then being a bogey 5 on the card).

Freddie Ball arrived on the 18th tee with 33 points, and no stroke, aware that something extraordinary was required. After a satisfactory drive, he played his second spoon shot into the green – and into the hole! Two for five points, and a tie. Not surprisingly Ball won the play-off. He also won the Kirby Cup and the Newbury & Crookham medal in the same year.

There were only ten competitors for the event – as at that time it was only the outright winner of the monthly medals or stablefords who qualified. Until 1971 they were played over a weekend and players could enter more than once, even on the same day. This had some benefit, one well known

Standing: George Adams, Len Moore, Jack Whiting, K. Swanson, Goring man, Marty Lewis,
Seated: Win Moore, Anne Moore, Rosilyn Whiting, Kathleen Graham, not known, Edna Simmons

member recalls, having entered in the usual way, blasting his first tee shot over the clubhouse. He then ran down to the foyer, entered the medal again, at three shillings, and returned to the tee to start afresh.

Wednesday medals, which now also count for the Rutherford Cup, did not start until 1975.

By the 1950s the ladies section had built up a strong membership, this being proved by the success of Mrs B. Simmons, sister of Mrs Jack Whiting, who won the Berkshire Ladies Championship in 1952, as a ten handicap player. She repeated this win in 1957, after moving to Sonning.

In 1957, Anne Coulman won the Welsh Girls Championship in its first year, being losing finalist the following year.

Two notable names were recorded in the club Junior Championships for 1957, Tim Greader winning with a gross 74. The runner up was Christopher Ball who, playing off ladies tees, returned a gross 87.

It is hard to imagine an AGM without some discourse on increased subscriptions, but the subject was never raised between 1955 (10 guineas) and 1962 (12 guineas). There was no evidence of an over 65s lower rate until after 1956 and country membership existed for those living outside a 20 mile radius.

There was a flicker of excitement in 1962 when proposals were made for a new clubhouse. The sites suggested were: ground between the 1st green and the present 12th green. (The 13th tee was not then in position), or, ground between the 13th and 18th fairways (opposite the tractor sheds). These proposals were taken to a special general meeting where they failed to gain approval. A similar proposition was made in 1967, when another site, land adjacent to the 14th tee, was added, but once again the members rejected the idea.

Club President Harold Bance presenting Jack Hughes with an illuminated address, in 1956, to commemorate his 25 years as club professional

"... We recall in particular the skilful tuition and the advice and encouragement you have at all times so willingly given, and by your cheerful example the manner in which you have enhanced the reputation of the club."

Short Game

1946

Whitlock having given a month's notice to the committee, the vacancy of greenkeeper arose. It was agreed that Frank Barton be asked to take this job at £5 per week for a period of 3 months. The position then to be reviewed.

The secretary to write a letter of appreciation to Whitlock for his loyalty to the club during the war years.

*

A cup given by Mrs Rutherford to be known as The Rutherford Cup is to be played for by the winners of the monthly Stableford Bogey Competition.

*

The secretary to get lamps for both locker rooms, if necessary to buy new ones.

1948

Jack Hughes was interviewed and asked if he would replace the steward and stewardess.

Although he was willing it was decided that as the club premises would be left unoccupied at night this was not a good idea.

*

Frank Barton, the greenkeeper reported that he could not carry on cutting the greens under present conditions and that some assistance must be given or he would have to hand in his notice.

The committee were informed that Jack Hughes was cutting the 15th and 14th greens, and cutting the fairways when time permits.

*

Correspondence between Mr Povey and the Secretary was read and Mr Ball was instructed to see Mr Povey regarding the loss of his shoes.

1949

The committee agreed that the club pay for a pair of Dunlop nailed shoes, value 37/3d to be purchased from the professional's shop to replace the old shoes lost by Mr Povey.

*

Professionals remuneration to be kept at £3.10.0 subject to some work being done to the bunkers when time allows.

*

The Air Ministry expressed sympathy towards the club and had agreed figures submitted to them for the reinstatement of the course.

The sum of between £1,400 and £1,500 had been agreed for the 1st hole.

The sum agreed for the 14th & 15th was £2,840.

A further sum of £100 to be paid to the club for delay in payment for the first hole, as the golf club had suffered by this hold up.

The suggestion of forming a table tennis section and joining the league was turned down in view of the lounge having to be used for the matches.

*

The firm of Allied Advertising Ltd having offered to provide the club with table lighters free of any financial obligation, it was agreed to accept.

*

14th hole – the secretary reported that the concrete could be moved by the end of the month.

*

A suggestion that a bar billiards table be installed was not accepted.

1950

The secretary reported that he and Mr Povey had seen Mr Bolton re the Crookham Cups that he holds but that at present he was not willing to part with them.

*

The secretary to see the steward and try to arrange for the price of sandwiches to be reduced to 3d each.

*

W.K.T. Hope (6) offered to play anyone off handicap, for his set of Gene Sarazen clubs, valued at £7, for double or nothing. The challenge was taken up in April by Mr R. Morrison (8) who was defeated by 3 & 1.

*

Damage being caused by the Craven Hunt that rode over our 14th green, a letter to be sent asking them not to hunt over the golf course.

1951

A vote of thanks was accorded to Mr Hobling for the bar billiards table.

*

... they were satisfied with the work of the steward but did not think that his wife had pulled her weight on the matter.

*

If no expense is involved the secretary to try and get ice cream supplied to the club for sale.

*

Clifford Cup In view of the fact that a service member has won this cup, it was agreed that this cup does not go to a service establishment.
The captain to see the winner concerned and explain the position.

1952

Bar billiards table. This has been given to the Boys Holiday Camp.

*

Mr W. Clinch was elected an honorary member.

Sunday saw the end of the old road across Greenham Common. A small silent crowd was on hand to witness the sorrowful sight of a bulldozer heaping up earth to a height of eight or nine feet across the road. (This was at the junction of Pyle Hill and Burys Bank Road, where the "peace women" camped, and at the opposite end, near Crookham House). *Newbury Weekly News*

*

Agreed that Jack Hughes be made an honorary member of the club for his long, loyal and willing service.

1953

After much discussion it was proposed by Mr Huxtable, seconded by Mr Bostock, that a men's only bar be made at the club. This was carried by 8 votes to 2.

1954

Damage to the 'men only' bars' outside wall by a member's (female?) car was reported. Mr Ball to see the member concerned.

*

Ladies pram shed. Proposed that the Ladies be given a separate portion of the present pram shed.

1956

It was reported that Americans were bringing their cars on to the 15th hole for the purpose of watching baseball. A letter to be sent to the Air Ministry requesting them to carry out repairs, and erect fencing.

1959

The steward be instructed that no personal loans be made to club members in future.

1960

The town clerk to be asked to have the gypsies removed from the borders of the course.

*

Fruit machines in the club lounge to be adjusted more favourably.

1961

Club football pools. Mr Rodford reported a profit of £69.8.1. He agreed to run the pools for another year.

1962

The suggestion from C & S Enterprises of London, to have games of chemin-de-fer at the club was not thought practical.

9

Course and Clubhouse 1963 – 1973

In three successive years from 1957 the Dunn Trophy was won by L.J. (Chuff) Stradling with scores of 145, 148 and 161. F.N. Ball won in 1960 and R.J.K. Horn in 1961. Stradling had a fourth success in 1962 (149). They were all fine players, and worthy champions, but thanks partly to the skilful tuition of Jack Hughes, there followed an explosion of talent.

Previous chapters of this book have acknowledged the high standards of George Wathen, W.K.T. Hope, and others who, individually, may have been as talented as the young pretenders who were to rule for the next ten years, and who displayed a measure of ability and attitude that brought honour and pleasure to the club: Chris Ball aged 18, Geoff Miller(18) and Peter Cronin (15). All were full-time students, following which they each went into full-time employment.

Ball and Miller had each won trophies in 1962, and 1963 opened with a win for Ball in the Kirby Cup with 72-6=66, one shot better than Miller, who reversed the result in the Dunn Trophy, beating Ball by one shot with 154.

Both players reduced their handicaps to five during the year, and represented the Berks, Bucks & Oxon colts team.

Ball (3) opened 1964 with a stableford score of 43 points, and proceeded to win the Dunn Trophy, the Kirby, the Elkington, and was in winning partnerships in the fourball, foursomes, and Captain and Pro cups. These results also earned him the Masters Trophy. By the end of the year he was off scratch.

Until 1965 the Dunn Trophy was won by the best gross score from those competing in the

Chuff Stradling with Jack Hughes

Four times Open Champion Bobby Locke partnered Tim Greader in a 2/1 victory over Jack Hughes and Chris Ball in an exhibition match in 1964, in aid of the Red Cross. Locke was round in 68

Fairhurst Cup. In the afternoon of the Fairhurst, Ball equalled the amateur course record with 65, and later won the Dunn with 73+71=144. Peter Boynton was second with 72+74=146.

Ball started 1966 with an early 66-1=65, but it was Miller's turn to be club champion. He scored 144, Ball finishing second, one shot behind. Peter Boynton was third with 78+70=148.

Peter Cronin arrived on the scene by winning the Newbury & Crookham Medal, and he pushed Ball to the limit in an exciting Ronaldshay Cup final. He was three down after five holes of the second round, but played the next ten holes in two under par, to be three up with three to play, only for Ball to square the match with a 4 at the 36th hole, and win it with another at the 37th.

At that time the Ronaldshay and Elkington Cups were handicap events run throughout the summer, each attracting the same large entry. For a player to reach both finals in the same year was a considerable achievement, but this Cronin did. Having already lost one final, he was probably apprehensive about facing Miller in the other, despite receiving two shots per round. The match was all square after 18 holes, Miller going round in 70 to Cronin's 73. Cronin had been three up after 13 holes but Miller came back to all square by playing the last five holes in 17 shots. In the afternoon Cronin gained an early advantage and ran out winner by 4 and 3.

It normally takes one day to win the Dunn Trophy, but in 1967 it took Geoff Miller one month, play being washed out after the first round in June. He carried forward a 69, and added another in July, to retain the championship with 138. Cronin was runner up with 69+70=139, with Ian Dyke and H. Richardson equal third on 142.

The final of the Fourball Cups saw Ball (1) and Tony White (8) beat Cronin (3) and Miller (2) by 8 & 6 over 36 holes. This was an outstanding performance, the net betterball scores were 61 against 64 in the first round, and 33 against 41 for 11 holes in the afternoon. The card below shows the morning round net score of Ball and White, readjusted to the present order of play.

4 3 3 4 3 3 4 3 3 – 30
4 3 3 4 4 3 3 2 5 – 31

It was assessed that Ball scored a gross 66.

In the same year Cronin (5) won the Fairhurst Cup with scores of 68+64, and the following month won the Rutherford Cup with 37 points, off 4 handicap, with only 23 putts.

These two victories paved the way for Cronin to win the Masters Trophy, with a further four runner up positions.

Cronin started 1968 with three early gross scores of 68, 70 and 68 and, with his father Tom, won the Family Foursomes Cup for the third time in four years.

Peter Cronin on the 18th, having holed out for a record 63 in 1968, acclaimed by Peter Boynton

Ball (2) won the Fairhurst Cup for that year with net scores of 67+66=133, Roy Bishop (9) coming second on 61+74=135. Bishop had played an excellent morning round of gross 70 to lead by six shots, but Ball, as he does so often, saved his best until last, and was leader in the clubhouse. Bishop needed to finish with a 3 and a 4 to tie, but lost a ball on the 17th, and finished 5, 4. Ian Dyke scored an eagle two on the 10th (8th) in the morning round.

The Dunn Trophy for 1968 produced a memorable day for a variety of reasons. The news spread across the course like a forest fire that Peter Cronin had set a new amateur course record of 63, with two nines of 32+31 (on today's order of play this would be 30+33). He had five birdies, and only one bogey, at the last hole. Ball with 68 and Miller with 69 made up the final trio for the afternoon round, but Miller started 5, 6, and was soon out of serious contention.

After six holes Cronin, one over par had increased his lead to 6 shots, but by the 9th (7th) this had been reduced to 3, and he dropped another shot at the 12th (10th) which Ball parred.

The 13th proved to be the vital hole, Cronin taking six, and Ball holing a chip for a three to take the lead. This devastated Cronin who slumped further behind, finishing with 82 to 72 by Ball, the winner by five shots. Cronin, incredibly, had played the first 24 holes in three under par and the last 12 in 14 over. Miller was third with 146, one shot behind Cronin.

Ball was later to win the Fairhurst Cup to complete the "double", but through his consistent prominence Cronin took the Masters Trophy for the year.

The club team won the Reading & District Foursomes league for 1968. The players involved were:

Chris Ball	8 games	+ 29 (holes up)
Ian Dyke	3	+14
Geoff Miller	9	+7
Tim Greader	9	+7
Peter Boynton	10	+6
Rex Hepburn	7	-12
Peter Cronin	9	-17

Mike Powell and Stan Reeh also played.

Newbury & Crookham Foursomes League winners 1968
Left to right C.J.Ball, M.Powell, P.Cronin, R.Hepburn, P.Boynton, T.P.Greader, G.W.Miller, S.Reeh, I.Dyke

John Niven (4) disturbed the pattern when he beat Cronin (2) by two holes in the semi-final of the Ronaldshay Cup, which he went on to win. Cronin and Greader won the foursomes cup for 1968, an outstanding year, in which Ball and Miller made their full county debut.

The club team were successful in the 1969 Berks, Bucks and Oxon club championship at Denham. Representing Newbury & Crookham were: C.J. Ball 71+72 (143), G.W. Miller 77+74 (151) and P.T. Cronin 77+79 (156). Chris Ball tied with Michael King of Reading for the individual championship, but lost the three hole play-off by taking three putts on the last green.

Ball again won the Dunn Trophy with 68+70=138, Greader was second with 74+73=147 and J. Niven third with 76+74=150.

The winner of the Junior Handicap was 12-year-old David Niven with 96-30=66.

The play-off for the Captain and Professional Salvers provided a thrilling and unusual climax to the season. Tim Greader played a lone hand against the better ball of captain Jim Miller and Jack Hughes, who were simultaneously playing the better ball of Tom Pinnock and John Cole. Greader had played his challenge with Barry Williams who had since emigrated. The play-off was necessary because two pairs had beaten the captain and pro by the same score.

In a strong gale Greader performed well, and after 17 holes both matches were all square. Pinnock and Cole were each to receive a shot on the last hole, but they managed only a 6, net 5, matching the captain and pro and halving their match. Meanwhile Greader had hit two glorious woods to the green, and sank a long putt for a three, and a satisfying victory.

Cronin recorded a 65-2=63 to win the final medal of the year, and Miller won the first medal of 1970 with 38 points, gross 67.

An award was made to Chris Ball by the Berks, Bucks and Oxon Union of Golf Clubs in recognition of his county performances. He had played 29 singles and foursomes matches, of which 18 had been won, and one halved.

Cronin and Miller won the 1970 Berks, Bucks and Oxon Foursomes championship at Henley. After 35 holes they led Michael King and Ron Burgess of Reading by one shot, but on the last hole Burgess putted successfully from 15 feet for a birdie four to force a three hole play off over the 1st, 2nd and 18th holes. The first two were halved in par, and on the 18th Cronin pitched close enough for Miller to win the match with a birdie putt.

During 1970 Miller began living and working in London and applied for country membership. He was to appear less frequently and was gone from the scene by 1976/7.

Chris Ball was beaten into second place by Michael King of Reading in the Berks, Bucks and Oxon county championships at Maidenhead. King 73+75=148, Ball 73+77=150. Newbury were second in the team championships. Ball followed this one week later with a record win in the Dunn Trophy, 65+69=134.

John Niven and Bert How tied for second place with 143 followed by Miller with 145 and Cronin with 147.

This was the first year that the Dunn Salvers were introduced, presented by Peter Boynton and Chris Ball, one each for handicap groups 4-9 and 10-18. The idea was to boost interest in the Dunn Trophy day, which it immediately did. There was a play-off over three holes for the 4-10 category between Niven and How. After halving the first two holes they were playing the 13th where How reached the front of the green for three and Niven had put his second on to the first tee from where he pitched in for a 3.

The progress of the Newbury "triumvirate" who had dominated the scene since 1963 was not without threat. Players such as Ian Dyke, Tim Greader, John Niven and Bert How were continually recording low scores which in other times would have brought more success.

Bert How (4) won the Newbury & Crookham Bogey on 5 up, with a gross score of 65, and nothing worse than a 4 on his card.

Tim Greader (4) partnered 17 year old Carl Mason (2) in the Newbury men's open meeting, leading the field in the morning with a net 67, the afternoon with net 62, and taking the all-day prize with 129.

Newbury & Crookham won the Reading & District Foursomes league in 1970. Those who represented the club were:

G.T. Blake	10 matches	+26 (holes up)
T.P. Greader	9 matches	+25
P.T. Cronin	8 matches	+23
C.J. Ball	6 matches	+23
E. Howard	6 matches	+23
G.W. Miller	6 matches	+17
A.P. Boynton	4 matches	-9

Others: M.J. Powell 2+5, G. Woodfine 2+3, R. Williams 2+2, R. Morris 1+5, F.N. Ball 1+2, R. Hepburn 1+1 and I. Dyke 1-2.

Chris Ball scored one of his finest victories in winning the West of England Open Championship at Burnham and Berrow, beating Richard Eyles of Frilford Heath by 5&3 in the 36 hole final. He became the first Berks, Bucks and Oxon player to win the trophy which was inaugurated in 1912.

Peter Cronin began 1971 with a stableford score of 42 points, a gross 65, and again had a tense struggle with Ball in the Dunn Trophy. In the morning round Cronin had a lead of three shots, Ball taking a seven on the 18th hole. They were level with five to play, but Ball finished 4,3,3,3,4 which was too good for Cronin, Ball winning with 74+67=141 to Cronin's 71+73=144.

Ball had previously won the Portal and Fairhurst cups, and was runaway winner of the Master's Trophy for 1971.

Fifteen-year-old David Niven won the January medal in 1972 with 72-12=60, and Ball followed in February with 66-1=65.

Cronin and Greader won the Berks, Bucks and Oxon foursomes championship at Goring, and Greader took the Fairhurst Cup for the third time, having previously won in 1958 and 1960. Cronin (3) drew first blood in the cup competitions, winning the Portal (flag) with three shots left after 18 holes.

It may have been expected by 1972 that Cronin would never overcome Chris Ball in the Dunn Trophy and, ominously, Ball led the morning round

Peter Boynton demonstrating his golf, or fishing, grip to Freddie and Ruth Ball, his wife Betty,, and Jim and Brenda Miller, at the 1968 Ball

by one shot with a 69. In the afternoon Cronin played the steadier golf and had moved into a three shot lead after 13 holes. This time he resisted the usual late charge by Ball and won by two shots with 70+72=142. Surprisingly this was his only club championship win. In the following medal Cronin scored 66-3=63.

In assessing the quality of golf in this decade, perspective should be maintained. The course now has a par of 68, against 67 then, the 13th hole since being lengthened, by only 40 yards, but making that one shot difference. Many tees have been pushed back into corners and into trees, certainly increasing the degree of difficulty but, to counter that, equipment was very ordinary – there were no Big Berthas or Firesticks. Those who have played throughout the years since 1963 will be quick to testify how the rough has virtually disappeared since then, as have many encroaching trees and bushes.

In the Clubhouse

With such a high standard of golf being displayed on the course, not surprisingly the club was functioning well. Compared with any other period, this was probably the easiest for both the committee and the members. There were no major issues on the horizon, and those that were to follow were not forced upon the club.

The members 1968

Berks, Bucks and Oxon played the first ever county match at Newbury & Crookham in 1963.

Philip Greader retired as honorary secretary in 1965, after 20 years in office. His replacement, Mr C.S. Barron was the first paid secretary, employed on a part-time basis, at £400 a year.

Geoff Miller was awarded a golfing blue at Cambridge. He won both his foursomes and singles matches, a feat he repeated in 1966.

Peter Boynton put forward a proposal in 1966 for the formation of a foursomes league, to be played on a scratch basis. The clubs invited were Calcot, Emmer Green and Goring & Streatley. The Reading and District Inter-Club Foursomes League was started in 1967 and has flourished since, with Newbury & Crookham featuring prominently. Henley, Sonning and East Berks joined the league later.

Subscriptions took a sudden leap in 1966 from 13 guineas to 19 guineas, the over 65s (10% of the membership) being treated particularly well, with no increase to their 8 guineas.

Thanks mainly to the initiative of Alan Seward (captain 1974), the first match against a team representing Newbury Rugby Club was played in 1968. This has become a regular feature enjoyed on and off the course.

The clubhouse was altered in 1968-69, the dining room being merged with what is now the TV area, which was then the bar. Shutters were fitted between the two. Subscriptions were increased to £25, and the membership limit was raised to 520.

Miller, Ball and Cronin played in the 1968 English Championship at Ganton.

Mr C.S. Barron resigned as part-time secretary owing to ill health. His successor was Mr S.M. Wilson, a playing member of the club.

In 1969 arrangements were made for a practice area within Greenham Common Air Base opposite the car park. The concession was withdrawn after two years.

C.J. Ball played for Berks, Bucks and Oxon in the English County Championship at Saunton, which they won. Ball tied with Michael King of Reading for the individual championship, but lost in the play-off. A letter of congratulation was sent to Michael King from the club, on his selection for the Walker Cup in 1969.

Frank Shergold retired from the committee in 1969 after 22 years' continuous service. He was captain in 1958. He and F.N. (Freddie) Ball were elected honorary life members.

For the first time a qualifying round was introduced in the Ronaldshay Cup in 1969. A drop in the entries meant that this was not necessary in 1994 and 1995.

In 1971 S.M. Wilson resigned and George Adams became the first full-time secretary at £1000 p.a. plus £350 expenses. He was a former Newbury & Crookham member and had been a committee member, and captain of Reading Golf Club.

New changing rooms were built in 1972. The previous ones were on the site of the present secretary's office, being about the same width but protruding some 30 to 40 feet more towards the 1st fairway.

Country membership was discontinued in 1972.

Mr and Mrs Eric Blackburn won the Pellows and Gilroy Cups, the first time the "mixed double" had been achieved.

Members at the 1972 AGM rejected a proposal for an increase of £10 to the subscriptions but an amendment proposing an increase from £25 to £30 was carried by three votes. The following year there was another increase, to £35 (over 65s paid £12).

Centenary Year 1973

The first of the special events commemorating the centenary year was an 18 hole foursomes medal for The Dominic Trophy, a handsome silver cup presented by Peter Dominic Ltd., who were encouraged to do so by Bert

President Freddie Ball making the presentation to Jack Hughes, commemorating his 50 years at the club

How, then employed by them. The winners were Len Moore and Terry Howard (12) with a net 66. The format has changed over the years and it is presently played as an "aggregate fourball".

The club held its first ever pro-am tournament in May. Tim Greader, club captain and chief organiser of the event was unable to play through illness. His place was taken by Bert How, who won the 36 hole amateur scratch medal with 75+75. Other members to win prizes were John Niven, Phil Risby and Bob Bance.

In June the club entertained a party of visitors from America under the auspices of the People to People Sports Committee who were on their last stop following matches in Spain, Portugal, France, Switzerland and Germany.

As a gesture of appreciation the club received a large picture showing a number of scenes of Newbury, Massachusetts. The whereabouts of the picture is a mystery.

Also in June the new Centenary Salver, open to men and women and presented by Mr and Mrs F.N. Ball, was won by Richard Bates (11) who scored 40 points with a gross 73 in a field of 115.

The most ambitious, but no less successful undertaking, was the inter-club tournament which filled a whole week, Monday to Friday. Each of 12 clubs sent teams of five every day, one each for men 0-9, 10-18 and 19-24 handicaps, and ladies silver and bronze division. Four scores only were to count, with the fifth cards counting in the event of a tie. Newbury tied with Maidenhead but lost on the fifth cards.

The centenary of the club stems from the Crookham connection, but it is convenient that 1973 is also the 50th anniversary of the opening of the present course, and Jack Hughes had served the club through every year of it. A very busy week in July included the captain's, and the lady captain's days, and it was after the distribution of the captain's day prizes that a presentation was made to Jack and his wife Kit. Jack received a chiming clock and a cheque for £1,000, and his wife a Worcester tea set and tray. The president Mr F.N. Ball made the presentation. After thanking the members or their generosity Jack thanked his wife for her support, and made special mention of the "two Billys", Mr and Mrs W. Perry who had helped him so much in looking after his shop. (Bill Perry was captain in 1952.)

The ladies held a centenary inter-county tournament. Eight county teams played a 36 hole scratch competition which was won by Bucks with Surrey second, Hampshire and Wiltshire tying for third place. Other counties attending were Berkshire, Gloucestershire, Hertfordshire and Oxfordshire.

The ladies also held a centenary open meeting which attracted players from 14 clubs.

Two records were set on the course in 1973, Chris Ball, with the same partners, won the fourball (Gwyn Woodfine) and foursomes (Freddy Ball) cups, for the second successive year.

A. Panting won the two oldest cups, the Newbury & Crookham Bogey and the Newbury & Crookham Medal in the same year.

Peter Boynton was chairman of the centenary committee. The two captains, Tim Greader and Mrs June Worthington, were kept very busy, as was the chairman of the social committee Alan Seward.

Chris Ball

The Evolution of the Course
1923 – 1995

In 1991-92 Frank Barton was asked to write a series of articles for a club newsletter, and the result was a poignant, romantic history of the course, seen through the eyes of a member. As an introduction, he takes that member back to pre-war days in the following article.

Life of a Golf Club Member
by Frank Barton

Before covering the course, we will try to describe what life was like for a member in the pre-war years of 1923-39.

Our member would arrive at 10 o'clock (only tradesmen and servants were abroad before that) and carrying his leather bag of golf clothes would proceed to the changing rooms. Being the product of public school or army service he was a hardy soul or he needed to be, the old changing rooms being very cold and very spartan.

Concrete floors, wooden benches, cold water only in the taps, cold showers and no heating. Under these conditions he would change for golf and proceed on his way.

His caddy would be waiting for him having already been booked at the professional's shop.

Having completed his round he now returns to the clubhouse to change once more into gentleman's attire.

Ah! now for a drink. He has a choice, one large barrel of Worthington best bitter (drawn from the wood) the like of which I've never tasted since, or the usual shorts: whisky, gin, brandy, etc. No ice, no wine, no fruit machines, no central heating. If it was cold a big log fire was lit by the steward, where our worthy would stand with his rear end to it to get warm. Lamps were the paraffin variety, pulled up and down on long chains, but rarely needed – a log fire, good whisky, a circle of friends and tales to tell of battles and matches won and lost – who needed lights.

Having finished his drink, he would depart for lunch. Then all was quiet until the afternoon when at 2 o'clock those who were to play would arrive. Meanwhile, the pro and the steward would retire for lunch. The Secretary – I cannot say much, he was the Honorary Secretary, and put in only the occasional appearance working mostly from home. Mr Bloxsom was his name.

I have called our member "he" for my story because it was very much a male preserve, women we will say, were tolerated but golf was still looked upon as a game for the male, and the clubhouse was his "club" where he could drink and gamble away from the women. Oh yes! they loved their card games.

Women were not allowed in the bar or the men's clubroom. They did have a room to themselves though, and could have a drink taken in. For all this, approximately 120 members paid 6 guineas a year. They paid one penny for a score card which measured 6 inches across, to use to measure a stymie, and a penny booking fee for a caddie.

Caddies were in great demand and earned 2/6d (12.5p) per round. There were six regular full-time caddies and Saturday and Sunday would see 30 to 40 all waiting for jobs.

It was my job as assistant professional and caddy master to allocate the caddies to the members. The best caddies went to the best turns. Oh yes! a good caddie got 3/- or 3/6d and was asked for by the best players. The fee you see was 2/- (10p) plus tip, and we had a few who only paid this, so they got the novices and I got it in the neck.

It was the days of the great house parties when it was the done thing to bring all your Guests for a round of golf before lunch, and bookings of four or eight was the norm.

Then on Sunday afternoon the gambling fraternity would take over and oh boy! did they enjoy their golf. To name a few Harold Bance, Blink Legg, Bill de-Castro, Henry Wilson, Ken Hope.

They laid odds on every shot and every hole and were great fun to be with, then in to play cards for the evening.

Yes! I suppose there was a great dividing line between members and staff. It was always 'Yes sir!' or madam, but there was great respect on either side. We knew they had the power and the money to keep us in jobs and they knew that by our work and many like us, we kept them in a life style that they were born to.

All in all, they were a jovial crowd and each in our own way we were a contented lot.

So in a small way I have taken many older members down Memory Lane and hope I have made the younger ones realise things have changed for them for the better.

The Course 1923 – 1994

In tracing the evolution of the course, holes will be described in the order played today. Dominant throughout will be quotations from the articles by Frank Barton.

The 1st

Originally the tee was in the position of the present ladies tee. For a period in the 1970s the men's tee was between the oak tree and the holly bush, before being moved to its present position. The value of the cross bunkers has been queried, even as recently as 1994. They were not in place when the course opened. It was reported in 1931 "A new bunker is to be placed across the whole length of the bank, where the fairway starts at the 1st. It will add to the character of the hole, and improve the appearance of the entrance to the club".

The left fairway bunker was installed in 1936. The trees planted near the right hand bunker, and those leading from the pro shop to the tee, were planted in 1970.

FB: We will start at No 1 and stand with our intrepid golfer on the 1st tee, and what do we see? No line of protective trees on the right, but between us and the first line of bunkers stands a sea of waving grass, yes! waist high, one gang mower width path carved through its middle, so a topped shot – and a lost ball.

To the left where the small spinney now grows was the dreaded sewer beds, these were fenced in and "Out of Bounds". Having survived these hazards and placed a good drive up near the right and left bunkers we are now looking at an acre or more of solid concrete between us and the green.[1] This is the end of the old war time runway that went from here towards Kingsclere. Quite a carry because if you hit this you will hit the roof in more ways than one.

This was later dug out leaving an 18" deep pit of white gravel where many balls were lost against the glare of the stones. Over a period of two years this was filled and turfed and the outline can still be seen today.

Having reached the green, we now find it is a small newly turfed one with old fairway turf, cut with an ancient push mower, no water, and a putting surface leaving much to be desired.

The 2nd

Soon after the opening it was reported that "all the roots had been removed from the slope and 10,000 turves had been laid on the fairway, a haycutter was employed for five days, and youths had been utilised for raking up the hay".

FB: Some of you will remember it as No 4 but for our purpose we will take the holes as they are numbered now.

We will now go back to the 30s and ah! what a lovely sight we see as we stand on the tee. A golf hole carved out of a pine forest. Lovely firs to the right of us and to the left of us and at the end of the twin lines of trees the green. No wind, a lovely scent of pines, but don't dare pull or slice. A thick grass gully at the bottom with a stream flowing through. The colour of kingcups, buttercups, milkmaids, the flash of the dragon flies, one could hear all nature buzz and sing, but alas along came the second World War and Italian POWs cut every single one of these lovely firs for pit props. This left the land each side of 2 and 3 completely bare so our golfer of 1946 would now be looking at a sea of bramble bushes and stumps each side of his fairway. Nature took its course and along came myxamotosis, a nasty disease that killed off all the rabbits. It appears that unbeknown to us the little beggars had been eating off all the young trees that nature was providing, and lo and behold up through the brambles came a forest of young oak trees and today's golfer now plays through an avenue of them.

The small pot bunker in front of the green was put there by Mr P.H. Greader, reputably just beyond where his drive would reach, remember in those days the fairway had a coat of thick grass.

---

[1]In the suggestions book it was proposed that the broken concrete should be sprayed green, to cut down the time spent looking for balls.

The 3rd

When this green was constructed it was surrounded by several small bunkers. In 1928 some were taken away and others followed until, by 1960, they had all gone.

FB: Now we come to the 3rd and oh! what changes we have here. The pre-war golfer would have stood on what is now the ladies tee. To his right and left would have been woods of Scotch pine and Larch trees. The view between this avenue would have been straight across the field at the back of the green to the Kennet Valley and Thatcham, there being no trees in this area at all. As a matter of interest, it is all gravel and was covered in white stones, making the finding of one's ball very difficult. It remained this way until myxamotosis struck in the 1950s and up came the forest of silver birch you see today.

Well! back to the tee, and in front of us the ground levels out to form a plateau ending in a sharp drop to the valley in front of the green, through which winds a lovely brook, fed with clear spring water from our lovely common. In the wood on the left it made a pond round which grew blue iris, primroses and bluebells, also a water hole for wildlife. The green itself was known as the Hot Cross Bun green because it had two ridges built into it and one of my first jobs was to take the cross ridge out and with a wheelbarrow build the ladies' 4th tee with the soil. Incidentally, the small ridge at the back between the grass bunkers was put there by the workmen who, when building the green, had their soil tipped in the field at the rear and then wheelbarrowed it down into place.

Now! back to the tee and our golfer of 1946. His tee is being made bigger with rubble brought from Newbury Racecourse which was a war time storage depot for US Forces and to his right and left devastation, no trees, just brambles, all gone for pit props. Except! one lone tree that they did not want, the Turkish oak that stands today forward and left of the ladies' tee. I could have felled it then with a few strokes of a Bushman saw, and I wish I had – why? you ask, because without it the tees could have been extended and the hole kept its character.

Anyway must press on, the same happened each side as it did at the 2nd up through the brambles grew silver birch copses each side of our hole.

Now to our tale of woe. Where, you may say, has our stream gone. Well, come 1952 and the construction of the airbase, the Air Ministry decided that the flow of drainage water from the runways would be so great that it would wash away the banks of our peaceful little stream, so they decided to pipe it. Then came the question of fill, what better than our plateau, so in came the bulldozers and you see the result today, not too bad except we lost the stream.

Well! we now have a lovely stand of birch trees to our left and along come the planners – "We want more length". So a huge swathe is cut through the birch wood and along came more bulldozers. You can all see today what you have got, a point for debate, about which of the two holes has most character.

The old hole was the prettiest, but that is a matter of opinion I suppose.

One more interesting point on this hole. The mature oaks that guard the green were wisely bought back by the committee of the day. When Captain Baxendale decided he was going to sell the course, he sold approximately 50 mature trees first. So committees do do the right things sometimes!

The 4th

FB: And so we come to Number 4 hole and what is known as the Bottoms. Not a great deal of change down here except before I note them I think I should describe some of the scenes of desolation that faced us after the war years.

An electric fence was placed across the top end of 4,5,7 and 8 holes turning the Bottoms into one vast field for the grazing of cattle, so what with them and the rabbits in sole charge for six years I think you can imagine what it was like.

There was thick matted grass everywhere, thistles 6 foot tall, ditches trodden in and blocked, and where you now have gullies and valleys was a sea of brown sludge and rushes.

It meant that the greens and tees had to be stripped of the rough matted grass, re-levelled, and turfed with turf cut from the few top fairways that had been spared (13 and 10 to be exact). All this with hand turfing irons (no turf cutting machinery in those days) and to haul it one old Fordson tractor, a home made wooden trailer about the size of a good box. The wheels had two tyres and no tubes. We stuffed them full of dead grass and sealed the holes in the tyres with old US Army issue gaiters we wrapped round with telephone wire.

Daily we had the help of ten German POWs who were willing workers but rather unskilled in the finer points of golf course construction.

I would like to mention now if it had not been for the drive and initiative of Mr P.H. Greader through that hard winter of 45/46 we would not have got those bottom holes back. He had many friends in the farming community of those days and he twisted their arms to procure all sorts of tools that we did not have – spike harrows, disc harrows, grass cutters, rollers etc. We tore it, we cut it, we raked it, we burnt it, we cursed it, and his battle cry was if we are not down there playing by Easter, Baxendale is not going to renew our lease. Well! it may have been a ploy, I do not know, but it got results and we opened up with the Fairhurst Cup. The greens left much to be desired but the fairways were quite good.

Well, to get back to the holes, Number 4 was much as it is now except for the large tee, and the rough from tee to fairway was knee high stuff, also the poplar trees were not there and of course through the wood on the left and across 5 fairway there was a deep open ditch.

The 5th and 7th

FB: This was a little more formidable, there being a deep open ditch and rough grass between you and the fairway, on the left to the right of the big oak tree was a massive bunker and to our right where now grow the poplars were two sets of huge bunkers shaped like lamb chops so one caught your drive from 5 tee or the other your second shot from 7.

The bunkers Frank refers to were installed in 1931. Another intention – to install a bunker across the whole width of the fairway, along the ridge, was not proceeded with.

The 6th

The hole was constructed with a round, not a pear-shaped, green, with two small bunkers, one at each back corner (see photo, 1923). Later "to prevent the slice from getting a flukey run up to the pin", a bunker was set along the left-hand side of the green. By 1950 the pear shaped green had been constructed, and the bunker extended to cover the whole left side. It was divided, once by 1954, and again in later years.

The 7th

When constructed, this hole had an open ditch across, in front of the green, where there is now only a double ridge. In 1928 the minutes indicate that it was to be covered with 3/4" wire netting, and treated as a hazard.

> FB: On to the 7th and the huge pit that was dug out to build the 6th green (with wheelbarrows) is now filled in with the new 7th tee.
>
> Away down the fairway and yes! the dip and bank that runs across was once an open ditch to catch your second shot, but the fall was so bad that it was all sludge and rushes instead of a flowing stream, so we diverted it and piped it in lower down near the green.
>
> Ah! now the green, the older members will have memories of this, the original was at ground level with a bank at the back. Needless to say this held the water and after a heavy storm the green became a lake.
>
> So Mr Greader decided we would raise it up and he wanted a replica of the 3rd green at Wentworth. So to Wentworth we both went, armed with note books and pens, measuring tapes and a lot of cheek. Back we came set to work with a will that autumn, and I am quite proud to say we did produce an exact replica of that same green, but Oh dear! the members did not approve. That same green at Wentworth has now been reshaped as even the top pros could not handle it.
>
> Many will remember it being a plateau green, the back half 5 foot higher than the front half, with a steep wavy bank across centre like a waterfall making a difficult uphill putt and hard to judge the line.
>
> Many the secret smiles we had watching the balls just reach the top and then roll all the way back.
>
> Anyway as soon as Mr P.H. Greader retired, the call went out "Frank get that green rebuilt", it was duly done and you now have your present one.
>
> The ditch to the right was re-aligned, the banks sloped and of course the old black barn and stable was demolished, a haven in many a storm.

The shed referred to is visible in the picture from 1950. Demolished in 1971, it was said to be over 100 years old but had become unsafe. Many a player had profited from seeing the ball bounce from its roof, on to the green.

The 8th

> FB: The changes here are mainly the ditches or should we call them streams. Our pre 1946 golfers would be faced with a stream running down the centre of the fairway in a line from the corner of the wood, where it can still be seen, to the gravel bridge you now cross in front of the tee. It was not too deep and very pretty with a red flag placed half way so a drive that went in beyond the flag gave you a free lift out.

[1]Revised local rule: "A ball played from the tee which finishes beyond the flag, or within one club length of the ditch running along the fairway, may be lifted and dropped on the left side of the ditch without penalty.

Well! along came the War Agricultural drainage people and offered for free to move our stream so Mr Greader had them dig a very deep ditch all down the side of the hedge and down by the tee and across 7 fairway. It proved quite a hazard but luckily when they built the Bury's Bank Road alongside 14 they uncovered a double length of concrete pipes which we soon spirited away to find their last resting place at the bottom of the ditch; a small bulldozer and you now have a full width fairway.

Now up to the base of the hill. It was open streams much as you see it now, but! it was the long hot summer of 1947. The course was brown to a cinder, no water of any sort, greens, tees, fairways and rough, no mowing, so Mr Greader, never one to be idle, said we will pipe all this, even part of the beds, fill in and make a nice  wide fairway. This was duly done and mowed as such.

Well! roughly 30 years did roll away and now his son, Mr Tim is captain, and he says "Frank, the wheel has turned full circle – we will open up these streams, bring in the diggers, pull out the pipes". It was duly done and you now have the streams again.

Now with bated breath we await the year 2007 and who knows what that holds in store.

The 9th

FB: Here the ladies have moved back quite a lot from where you can still see the old ladies tee. Judging by the number of holes where this has happened the fair sex were once the gentler sex. No more it seems.

Not a lot of change at the green and except the two huge bunkers, one on the left and one on the right are done away with, for very good reasons may I add, in 1950.

The left-hand one was built over a spring which fed sand into the very extensive drainage system in front of the green, and the one on the right was in the wrong place.

The 10th

FB: The big change here is the causeway, (1961). It was a real killer on a hot day when you went down a rutted path over a sleeper bridge and then the long climb up the other side. The hill to the right of the 10th tee where we gouged out the fill for the causeway was all heather in those days, no trees at all.

Well, when the pipes were delivered to pipe the stream we unloaded them on the top of the hill so as we could roll them down one at a time to the bottom of the gully. So I reported to Mr Greader "Sir, the pipes have come for 10th gully." "Good! good!" he said, "The committee are having a meeting tonight to see if they can afford to buy them so get them in." Oh we loved it.

Of course our pre-war green was a lot nearer. As you traverse the fairway you will see a half-moon-shaped ridge. This was the back of a huge bunker, the green being in the centre and another bunker on the right. So quite a bit of length has been added.

The 11th

FB: I must say that this hole must have had the least of all change. The trees on the right are an added feature (1970) where once it was all rough grass and of course the valley on the left is now a coppice of trees where once only heather and wild strawberries grew in abundance. Of course this was all brought about by myxamotosis killing off the rabbits and allowing the trees to come up through.

The 12th

Originally a straight hole, it was given shape in 1970 when the poplars were planted in front of the large bunker guarding the green. This was made more impressive in 1995. Players are encouraged to drive up the left side, where the fairway has been redirected, making a more interesting hole.

The 13th

FB: Ah! we have some changes here. Of course most of you will remember the old boundary fence and how we acquired the piece of common and so extended the tee, but how many remember our formidable gully. Not just clouting a good drive down the middle and never mind how far it went. Oh no! It took a controlled shot with an iron to the edge and hope to carry it with your second shot, because if you were in it you were in trouble.

To start with it was a very deep gully with an open stream running right through the middle, a stiff climb out up the bank the other side, and a growth of grass and weeds that was almost tropical.

Ah! you say, how come it got like it is today.

Well the first start was when the airbase was to be built in 1952, the engineer officer in charge of Ops played golf and as you know they don't do things by halves. He said "Feller, I've got tons of concrete to get rid of, I'll fill that little ole gully in for you".

Well we could not afford pipes so from the first load of slabs we place the best ones alongside the ditch and others over the top forming a tile drain. Then down came the earth movers with their loads of broken slabs as big as table tops, non stop day in and day out. We reduced the depth by half and got to the bottom by the wood. Then the fun began. As you all know it gets very wet down here so one of these huge earth movers gets bogged down to the axles. Another tries to pull him out and he gets bogged down, and so does a third. By now we have a queue of very expensive vehicles waiting to dump their loads, work on the base comes to a standstill, so someone wants to know. Down comes a very high ranking officer. When he saw what he saw, he blew his top. The air was blue and heads were going to roll. The outcome was that they were to get the hell out of there and never come back. It appears they should have been filling in one of the gullies on the common.

Well! here we are faced with a sea of concrete slabs and the holes between, a graveyard for lost balls, and the sky the limit if you hit them. They stayed like this for quite some time and then by a stroke of luck Mr Barlow opened a new sand pit at Hermitage and let us have all the top soil. It was dumped in 4 cubic yards heaps all over the gully and Walt Freemantle and I spread and raked every load by hand (it took us weeks) and then seeded it. The next phase, in 1970, was a bulldozer which shaved off the steep ridge, and so you have the nice gentle gully that you know today.

Secretary Philip Greader with club member, Jimmy Harrison, in front of the 13th Green. Frank Barton is on the tractor (early 1960's)

In May 1936 a rule was passed as follows: "If a ball is lost in the 13th gully, another ball may be dropped behind the main ditch. Penalty, 1 stroke.

The 14th and 15th

FB: To conclude my story of the history of the making of our course, I will turn the clock back to the spring of 1946 and will recall a moment when Mr P.H. Greader and I stood on the 14th, the tee side of the gully and gazed towards what is now the green. What a barren and desolate scene we did behold. I shook my head and said "No! it will never be a golf course again." He, being the eternal optimist, said "It will you know!"

Well! we were standing by a barbed-wire fence that went across the fairway and the gully, as you know, was half full of old tyres, oil drums, wood, tin. All the debris of a war time airfield. There was a gravel road went from the big house and out round by the bungalow to the old control tower. Beyond that was a great expanse of gravel, concrete, taxi strips with a scattering of Nissen huts, tin huts and old gliders. No boundary, no road, and no vegetation, and money in very short supply.

First we cleared the gully, then we piped and filled the very deep ditch that ran right across the 14th fairway.

As a matter of interest, the pre-war golfer had to drive over this ditch which was so deep it was covered with poles and wire netting.

Then we pulled down the huts, and made good use of the tin and timber in repairing our own sheds.

Then a new concrete breaking machine wanted somewhere to demonstrate to Air Ministry officials its ability to smash up war-time airfields – what better place – so it was done. (1949).

Now the "wheels in wheels" swung into action, Newbury being more of a tight little community than it is now.

Big housing estates were going up. They wanted hard core for roads and we wanted top soil. A massive operation swung into action and our base for operations soon took shape. The hard core went and was replaced with top soil, which was duly spread to form two fairways, then some dubious looking turf was purchased and laid.

Now the problem of the greens, well! the pre war 14th green was a good chip shot farther on than the present green, and the old 15th was over in what is now the baseball field beneath the beech tree which still stands. (They were then par 5 and par 4.)

The new owner of the land, Captain Guy Baxendale, had other plans and he restricted our boundaries to short of the public footpath and the present fence near the 15th green.

The sites were duly chosen and the greens built as you know them today.

I will not dwell long on the construction of those greens but enough to say they were both put in the hands of a contractor, and both were a total disaster, so much so that we took them out of their hands and built them ourselves. The turf for 15 was cut from 2 squares to the right and left of the approach to 12 green. The outline still shows and I have still got the blisters. I cut every single one with a hand turfing iron.

As no doubt many of you remember, the post war 15th hole was designed from what is now the ladies tee. The men's medal tee and fairway were carved out of a belt of trees and concrete in later years (1973), which still gives cause for debate. Is the angle of the green right for the layout of the hole?

In 1952 the course was purchased by the members, so we were able to fence the boundaries and feel more secure in what we did. Of course that was the year the big bomber base as you know was commenced and so Bury's Bank Road was built making access to the club a lot better.

The 16th

FB: This was a slightly more difficult hole in the old days. The tee was farther back. Remember the 15th green was way over in what is now a sports field, and an open stream ran through the centre of the gully, also on the top left hand corner where the half moon bunker and the little spinney stands, there was a truly magnificent beech tree. This made the hole a true dogleg. Where did it go! Well! as I said at the beginning, the war-time runway traversed from No 1 fairway towards Kingsclere, so our lovely old tree was right in the flight path. Down it had to come, and if you look closely at the firs in the old gardens just beyond the fence you will see where they cut the tops out, and they have sprouted again.

The 17th

FB: No big change, let's keep it that way.

The 18th

FB: No major changes here. The tee is farther back from the old days and we made the cross bunker from one long one into 2 smaller ones (1977). Of course the line of very tall elm trees that once graced the side of the road by 18 green have long since gone, and you now have the hedge.

Having acquired extra land behind the 18th tee an experimental tee, a further 40 yards back, was being constructed during 1995 with a view to making the hole into a par 5.

11

Recent Years 1974 – 1995

Elsewhere in this club history there is a predominance of facts and figures relating to men. The reason, and excuse, for this is that there is more information available regarding men's golf.

Handicap golf, though the life blood of the club, conveys little about the relative merits of individual performances. This lack of perspective has stifled the story of golf in the ladies section.

Before the Second World War, Miss M. Stokes was the only player to attain a single figure handicap, her lowest being seven.

Neither Mrs Edna Simmons (1952) nor Miss Ann Coulman (1957) were single figure golfers when winning their respective championships, described earlier, although Mrs Simmons had briefly played off nine in 1951. There is no evidence of another lady being in single figures until Airlee Dyson (1967), and, in the early 1970s came Pauline Brown, Ann Thomas, Nicola McCann and Stephanie Jolly. Significantly, the ladies scratch championship was started in 1972, when Anne Thomas won with 78+84=162, 12 shots ahead of Mrs Margaret Pearn.

In 1967 Airlee Dyson became the first Newbury & Crookham girl to play in the British and English Girls championships, following which she was invited by the LGU to join its winter training programme.

Newbury Ladies won the Duncan Trophy and the County Shield in 1972, under the captaincy of Mrs Jane Freemantle (now Mrs Goodenough).

Anne Thomas retained her scratch championship in 1973. In 1974, 14-year-old Stephanie Jolly won it with 85+81=166, and again in 1975 with 80+82=162.

Newbury Ladies won the 1976 Cancer Relief Challenge Shield, which is open to all clubs in England. It was awarded to the club returning the eight best medal rounds in one day. The eight successful players, whose cards were 40 under par, were: Sarah Jolly, Ruth Ball, Wendy Marchant, Helga Pearce, Betty Part, Mary Baldock, Heather Howard and Janette Jolly. The Lady Captain's Rose Bowl was presented by Mr Cyril Goodenough in 1978.

Stephanie Jolly, whose achievements had brought pride and prestige to the club, became a professional (or "pro-ette" as they were known) in 1979, the same year that saw the arrival of 14-year-old Karen Davies from

Wrexham. Already of obvious talent, she developed further at Newbury, until she accepted a golfing scholarship in America in 1984.

When Newbury & Crookham ladies played in the final match of the 1979 county Fourball League, misfortune struck when Janette Jolly pulled a muscle after five holes, and was unable to continue. Her partner, Betty Boynton, gamely held on to halve the match for a vital point. Newbury & Crookham won the match, and the league.

Anne Thomas became the first Newbury & Crookham member to be elected Berkshire ladies captain in 1984.

In 1991 the lady president, Emily Southern, presented the Southern Vase, to be played for annually on president's day.

Grace Bradley and Gill Bowness won the Crookham Foursomes in 1994, with a net 72. Grace, 82, drove 60 miles from her south coast home in Highcliffe to play. She has played golf since the late 1940s, and joined Newbury & Crookham in 1968. Now off 30 handicap, she travels to play at Newbury about once a month, but averages three games a week at Highcliffe, mostly with men.

On the Course

A new name appeared on the Dunn Trophy for 1974, 17 year old David Niven winning with 145 from Peter Cronin, Brian Bowness (146) and Geoff Miller (147). C.J. Ball, captain for the year, was unable to play, due to a back injury which was to trouble him frequently.

The centenary pro-am tournament having been so successful, another was played in 1974, this time with a few celebrities, including England cricketer Ken Barrington and golfers Denis Durnian, Peter Alliss and Max Faulkner.

By 1975 the balance of power had changed, Cronin having slipped up to 5 handicap and Miller having moved away. Ball became less involved and won only five major club events over the next 10 years, compared with 27 over the previous 12. Meanwhile David Niven had won his first club championship and Roger Miles had arrived from Dorset (county champion 1982 and 1983). Miles had become reinstated as an amateur after a period as an assistant professional.

John Niven, Bert How and Tim Greader were ever present to push all others to their limit.

Greader had his only success in the Dunn Trophy in 1975 with 69+70=139. He led Miles by one shot after 18 holes, but Miles only managed a 78 in the afternoon – an unusual round which included seven penalty shots.

The following year, 1976, Miles was again involved in the tussle for the Dunn, sharing the lead after 18 holes, on 71, with Chris Ball. David Niven, Peter Cronin and Bob Gill were all on 72. In the second round Ball played the first nine in one under par, two better than Miles, and he held this lead to win with 71+67=138, with Miles second on 71+69=140.

Bert How won the 1977 Dunn Trophy with 67+75=142, four shots clear of David Niven and Peter Cronin. He was then aged 57.

It was no surprise that Stephanie Jolly won the Junior Handicap Cup with 68-2=66. David Rosier (17) was runner up with net 69. Stephanie's golfing progress is described in detail elsewhere. It is a sad fact of club life that only a small percentage of members would have seen her play, or played with her. A larger gallery of spectators than usual turned out to watch a final of rare quality for the junior matchplay championship cup, between 17-year-old Stephanie (1) and 14-year-old David. He had earlier beaten her in the junior scratch cup with a 71 to her 73, and had reduced his handicap from 17 to five in one year. In this final Stephanie was giving one shot, which proved a deciding factor, David winning on the last green.

Roger Miles won the Newbury & Crookham Bogey, going round in 66 to finish three up.

On New Year's Eve 1977, the captain, A.H. Martin, introduced a new winter competition, later labelled "the international", with competitors divided, as near as possible, into national teams. This has maintained its popularity since, and the club provided a trophy for the event in 1993.

Jack Hughes won the Division A medal in June 1978 with 72-5=67, reducing his handicap to four. Jack, then aged 70, was enjoying his first year of club competitive golf since he was a junior in the early 1920s.

John Niven won another June medal with 65-3=62, dropping two shots in the last three holes, and son David scored 66-2=64 in the August medal.

After one round of the 1978 Dunn Trophy, Peter Cronin, 72, led by one shot from Chris Ball, with Roger Miles on 75. After 35 holes all three, playing together, were level, but on the final hole Ball scored a 4 to his opponents' 5 to win with 145.

Represented by Miles, Cronin and the Nivens, Newbury & Crookham won the 1978 Ferndown Fox, a prestigious 54 hole men's invitation team event. This was the club's first, and to date only success in this competition.

Jack Hughes reduced his handicap to three by winning the November medal with 66-4=62 a score that was four under his age.

Roger Miles who had earlier won the 1979 May medal with 65 Scr=65 led the first round of the Dunn Trophy with 66, four ahead of the nearest challenger, John Niven. After 27 holes Niven had drawn level, but Miles went back into the lead after the 29th, and held it until the 34th where he dropped a shot to par. He dropped another on the 35th to go one behind. Niven was bunkered at the last with his second shot, but foiled Miles, who had made par, by getting "up and down" to win his second club championship with 70+73=143, becoming its oldest winner at 59. Miles was caught by David Niven, 73+71=144.

Late in the year, David Rosier scored 65-1=64 in a monthly medal.

Although the title of Master Golfer goes back to 1959, it was only in 1978 that £50 was set aside to purchase a Masters trophy.

The club, represented by Chris Ball, Roger Miles, John Niven, David Niven and David Rosier, won the 1980 Berks, Bucks and Oxon Club Scratch Championship at Maidenhead.

David Niven, having warmed up with 67-1=66 in the July medal, won the 1980 Dunn Trophy with 71+71=142 which was enough to beat Ball, whose morning round of 76 left him too much to do, by two shots.

The 1981 Dunn Trophy caused a buzz of excitement, and surprise, when the leader at lunchtime was 13 handicap junior Neil Birrell with 71. David Niven and Len Watkins were one shot behind. Neil had gone out early in the day and, perhaps mistakenly, did not wait to play in the final trio, which was his right, and was lost by the end of the day, which saw Niven win again with 72+69=141.

Roger Miles won the April medal in 1982 with 66-2=64, and led the morning round of the Dunn with 68, David Niven lying second with 70. Miles slipped out of contention through the afternoon and David Niven added a 71 for 141. John Niven, not in the first six after 18 holes, came through into second place with 76+69=145.

David Rosier returned 64-2=62 in the October medal.

In 1983 Len Moore donated The Win Moore Trophy in memory of his wife, an ex-captain and president, who died in 1982.

The Dunn Trophy for 1983 was won by David Rosier who led Chris Ball at lunchtime with 68 to 71. In the second round he did well to withstand exceptional golf from Ball whose four birdies and an eagle still fell four shots short of Rosier's total of 68+69=137.

The Dunn Trophy for 1984 was won by David Niven with 71+67=138. It was reported at the time that 67 was a new course record as this was the first year that the 13th was played as a par five, making the course a par, and SSS, 68. This record was to last for only one month, David Rosier scoring a gross 63 in the August medal.

A rare play off was necessary in the 1985 event after Len Watkins, handicap 6, having led the field with a 69, allowed David Niven to catch him in the second round, Watkins finishing 69+79 and Niven 75+73. Niven won the play off comfortably.

Niven was again the Dunn winner in 1986, with 68+71=139, beating John Claridge into second place by six shots. Claridge, a late starter at golf had made fast headway. Natural flair and hard work had made him a tough competitor.

New Order of Play

It was in 1985 that the holes on the course were re-numbered, after a trial period, a successful manoeuvre to enable the second starting hole to be at the halfway point becoming the 10th instead of 12.

It at last becomes possible to describe events on the course without adding a reminder in brackets of present numbers against original ones, as has been necessary in the entire story so far. Ironically, at this late stage, the chance may seldom occur.

Another innovation introduced in 1985 was that the Elkington Cup was changed to a scratch knockout event, Roger Miles becoming the first winner, beating David Rosier on the 37th.

David Harris was partnered by 12-year-old Nick Woodage in a 72 hole marathon. Playing with the two assistants, James Purton and Richard Howett they raised over £400 for the Golf Foundation.

The club revived its pro-am in 1986, after a 12 year gap. Richard Bates did most of the organising, as he has since, with notable assistance from his wife Bertha.

Winners of the Thames Valley Junior League 1986

Simon Lovell, Nick Woodage, Gareth Williams, Paul Phillips, Gareth Rowlands, Simon Butler, Wayne Collier, Tim Bune, Tim Butler

It was in 1986 that Karen Davies represented the British Isles in the Curtis Cup. Karen's golfing history is traced in another chapter.

In the 1987 Dunn Trophy David Rosier, with a 66, had a five shot lead going into the afternoon, his nearest challenger being Bert How on 71 and Chris Ball on 72. The final scores were Rosier 66+72=138, Ball 144 and David Niven 145.

David Rosier successfully won through, from the Open championship pre-qualifying round on Sunday and Monday of the Championship week at Royal Lytham. There he mixed with many famous golfers and scored well, but not well enough to progress into the Open championship.

Rosier finished second in the Memorial Trophy at Burnham and Berrow with 71-1=70 against a standard scratch of 74. This trophy is played off on the day preceding the West of England Matchplay Championship, and Rosier continued to play well, reaching the Sunday final, where he faced David Law from St Pierre. With eight holes to play Rosier was three down, but he fought back to be level at the 36th, and won the title at the first extra hole.

In the Ford competition of 1988 Rosier scored 67-1=66 but could manage only a 75 in the first round of the Dunn Trophy. Simon Butler led with 70, with Claridge 71 and Ball 73. Butler put his first tee shot of the afternoon into the front bunkers, and took 6, to a birdie by Claridge, which gave him a two shot lead which he held until the final hole where he picked up another shot to win by three with 71+73=144.

David Harris scored 66 in the pro-am and led for five hours, only to be beaten by one shot.

In June 1989, eight lady members undertook to play 100 holes in aid of the Battle Hospital Cardiac Fund. All were low handicap players, all cards were marked, and all holes completed. Play started at 4.45am, with a full set of caddies. They stopped for lunch, and snacks and finished just before 8 p.m. The players were Jill Edwardes, Gill Bowness, Jane Hall, Anne Hornby, Val Watson, Sandy King, Judith Sturgess (now Mrs Birch) and Jacquie Wailes.

Jill Edwardes scored a hole in one on the 17th, her 67th hole of the day. By the 95th there was a huge gallery and having played in two fours, the ladies came down the 100th hole, engineered to be the 18th, together, where there was much celebration. From there, after refreshing themselves, they went to the clubhouse for a cocktail party.

Jacquie Wailes recorded the lowest score, 459 gross. The total raised was £3,287.

John Niven took the Dunn Trophy for 1989 with 68+74=142, the morning score being under his age. He was four shots ahead of Tim Butler, Bob Williams and Kevin Dunks.

David Rosier was beaten on the 18th in the early rounds of his tenth successive English Amateur Championship.

There was a 54 year gap in ages when Tim Butler faced John Niven in the final of the Elkington Cup, in which youth overcame experience by 5 and 4.

David Harris won the Berks, Bucks and Oxon Professional Championships after a play off against Steve Watkins of Ellesborough, the home professional. Other names on the trophy include Max Faulkner and Jack Hughes.

David Rosier and Tim Butler tied for the 1990 Dunn Trophy, Rosier scoring 72+75 and Butler 74+73. Butler had taken 6 to Rosier's 4 on the final hole. In 1984 the play-off rules were changed; on this occasion it was over a four-hole circuit: 1, 11, 12 and 13. The first circuit was to be played out, with sudden death to follow. Butler took a two shot lead after birdying the first, which Rosier three putted. There were no further fluctuations and Butler took the title.

Ian Briggs played the final six holes in one under par in winning the 1991 Dunn Trophy by three shots from Tim Butler with 72+72=144.

Newbury & Crookham Juniors won the Thames Valley Junior League for the third time in 1991.

100 holes in a day - 1989

Val Watson, Anne Hornby, Gill Bowness, Jacqui Wailes, Jane Hall, Jill Edwardes, Judith Sturgess (now Mrs L.Birch), Sandy King

Scott Watson arrived at Newbury & Crookham, already a promising young golfer, and made steady improvement. He did not stay long enough to impose his name upon the club records, for in 1991 he became an assistant professional at Stoneham. He is now on the professional circuit.

Nick Woodage scored 65-5=60 in the Ford Medal of 1992, but was four shots short of Tim Butler's winning score in the Dunn Trophy, 74+71=145.

Julian Sandys won the 1993 and 1994 championships. In 1993 his morning score of 66 left his challengers, John Bowness, Nick Woodage and Brian Davies, three shots behind, and only Woodage stayed with him, but without finally closing the gap. Sandys added a 71 for 137 and Woodage a 71 for 140.

In 1991 Newbury & Crookham won the final of the Marston's Trophy for over 50's. The team, left to right: J.Scade, R.Heitzman, J.Calkin, J.Green, C.Arnold, B.Sturgess, B.Bowness, B.Haskell and B.Sloan. Forty-one clubs, mostly from Hampshire, had started the competition

In the 1994 event he again held off Woodage with 72+69=141 to 69+73=142. Tim Butler was third with 144. Butler was on summer holiday from America where he was enjoying university life through a golf scholarship.

In the 1995 Newbury & Crookham Bogey, Nick Woodage equalled the eleven year old course record of 63, held by David Rosier. This is the lowest score on the course since the order of play was changed.

The Dunn Trophy was brought up to date with overdue success for Brian Davies in 1995. The young favourites failed in the first round, and the final trio in the afternoon were Davies 67, Kevin Dunks 70 and Jason Axford 71. There were four others on 72. The scores were closer after nine holes, with Davies out in 37, Axford 35 and Dunks 34. Davies finished the stronger on 138, with Dunks on 140 and Axford on 142.

In the Clubhouse 1974-1995

The pressures of the centenary year may have proved too much for George Adams, who resigned as secretary whilst it was still in progress. Inevitably, for the first time, a full-time secretary, Sqd. Ldr R.J. Willams was appointed, but he died, in office, in 1976. His replacement was Ron Church, a 14 handicap member of North Oxford Golf Club, who was destined to remain much longer.

Subscriptions were raised in 1974 from £35 to £40, the over 65s concession being significantly altered from one third to one half. More noteworthy, however, was the introduction of the 5-day membership.

In 1975 the club bought the land behind the 14th green. Older members must have seen some irony in the situation, as the same land had been part of the golf course, laid out in 1923. When the course was bought from Mr Baxendale in 1938, its boundaries were altered, retaining some land to surround the lodge. That caused the shortening of the 14th and 15th holes. Committee minutes for 1975 show a suggestion that the 14th could be made into a par 5. Full circle. Fortunately nothing was done immediately and it was later exchanged, by arrangement with the council (1980), for the area which now contains the 13th tee, and the path from the 1st green to the 2nd tee, that whole corner being previously out of bounds. The exchange also gained the land now used for the large car park. Once again, in 1981, there were proposals for re-siting the clubhouse: "rear of the first green", "the copse adjacent to the 12th (10th) tee", "sheds site adjacent to 18th" and "rear of 14th". These suggestions failed, as before, but they triggered off moves to improve the existing premises and in 1982, under the guidance of John Trigg and the captain Fred Fisher, plans were laid for changes and additions which resulted in the present facilities, including the most evident addition, the secretary's office, and the front bar (1985).

There was a tragedy in 1985 when Michael Hutchins, one of our young greenstaff, had an accident whilst swimming on holiday in Portugal and was rushed home to hospital. The worst fears were realised and Michael has to this day been confined to a wheelchair.

Ron Church retired as secretary in 1989 after 13 years in office. He remains a playing member.

In 1987 Frank Barton was made an honorary life member. Frank, and his wife Hilda, were presented with wrist watches at a special occasion at the club to mark his retirement after 40 years' service as greenkeeper. The members presented the couple with a cheque for £5,000.

Lt Col. Tom Hutchison, former member of Newbury & Crookham, was secretary of Royal Lytham and St Annes from 1984 to 1988, during which time they hosted the Amateur Championship and the Open Championship. Although the golf was in the hands of the Royal & Ancient, Col. Hutchison and his staff were required to recruit over 700 volunteers for stewarding the Open.

He was also deeply involved in staging the Lytham Centenary celebrations in 1986.

In 1988 he moved to Huntercombe where he is still the secretary.

The year of 1990 will be remembered by all who were members throughout its traumatic summer. The greens were completely ruined by a mysterious gremlin in the watering system. All, that is, except the 3rd, which through a fault did not get "sprinkled" on the night the gremlins struck. At the time there were enough theories and remedies being promoted by a record number of experts in the club, to provide a whole chapter, or even another book. The course was closed in mid-summer and some competitions were held over to 1991, by which time the greens had made a remarkable recovery. As his year of captaincy was disrupted by these events, G.G. Woodage was offered another term, which he accepted in 1993.

With ambitious plans in hand for the course, including improvement to the sprinkler system, a new tractor, and a new vertidrain machine, the committee was looking for ways to raise capital in 1991. They devised a new life-membership scheme whereby members over 42 years of age, of ten years standing, could purchase life membership for £5,000. This was largely successful.

Greenham Common Airbase

In the book *Action Stations*, by Chris Ashworth, there is a sentence which reads: "Greenham Common airfield was first surveyed in 1941. Authority to requisition was given in May, and because the land was poor, there was none of the usual opposition from farming interests".

There is no evidence that the gentlemen of Crookham or Newbury District golf clubs made objections, and it is unlikely that they would have been heeded had they done so.

By the summer of 1942 the airbase was nearing completion, but by then it had been earmarked for USAF occupation. Flying began in November 1942, and the base was taken over by the Americans in October, 1943. Americans, for a while, seemed to have invaded Newbury but suddenly, in June 1944, they disappeared. The airborne troops assigned to the 438th TCG were all on base, which was surrounded by armed guards. "Overlord" was on, and General Eisenhower drove to Greenham Common on the evening of June 5th, to watch the first paratroopers leave on "Birmingham Belle", followed by another 80 C-47As, at 11 second intervals.

After the war there was strong local feeling that the common should be restored to its original condition and occupied parts of the Newbury course were returned to the club. The cold war of the 1950s prevented any further concessions. On the contrary, the complete rebuilding and extending of the base was completed by September 1953.

In June 1980 it was announced that Greenham Common would become a home for cruise missiles. Ninety-six were to be stored in purpose-built underground shelters (clearly visible today from the 14th hole). In the event of war, the missiles were to be dispersed in the surrounding countryside on trailers, from which they would be fired.

These activities exacerbated the situation at the gateways to the base, where the "Peace Campers", supported by the CND movement, had made their home.

With the end of the cold war, all military activity has ceased, and the Ministry of Defence is slowly releasing some buildings for business and leisure activities. The concrete is being broken up and eventually it is hoped that some of the land will be restored as "common land", although ironically an application from the club for a practice area, in 1993/94, was rejected.

The Americans made good use of Newbury & Crookham, taking advantage of special terms. Jack Hughes became their great friend, and he has a scrapbook of memories. Many USAF championships were played at Newbury. On one occasion the club acted as hosts to the wedding of an American couple, and Jack gave the bride away!

Many Americans won Newbury & Crookham competitions, the last to do so being Jodi Clor, who in 1991 fittingly won one of our oldest and most cherished trophies, the Newbury & Crookham Medal.

Short Game

1963

In view of the fact that the steward was in hospital again, it was agreed that they should be replaced as soon as possible. For the time being Jack Hughes was to be asked to help.

*

Agreed that the captain and secretary should see the steward to explain to him that he would be given notice, as he would probably be physically unfit to carry out the duties of steward.

The committee were prepared to pay him £100 if he vacated the cottage by the date given, otherwise he would get nothing.

*

Professional's practice shed. This to be painted by him as promised.

*

A new pro shop and pram shed had been erected and the car park cleared and tarmacked.

*

All members who have electric trolleys to be charged £1 per year if they charge batteries at the club.

1964

Agreed that F. Barton's wages be increased to £14.10.0 per week. Two members voted against the increase. (That being £1 only asked for, but 30/- given to him.)

*

Members to be urged to buy from their pro.

1965

The Sisters of Nazareth have asked for a subscription. It was agreed not to subscribe but to put the Sisters down for a competition.

1966

It was agreed that a telephone be installed in the secretary's office.

*

As a games licence would cost £100, the plans to run Bingo evenings were dropped.

1968

Mrs Ball showed the committee a silver brooch, presented to her, and for the use of future lady captains, by Mrs Moore.

*

Jim Miller, the incoming captain drove into the office on Sunday – no mean achievement as his backswing was greeted by an exploding rocket, the roar of a 12 bore shotgun, and the repeated firing of a starting pistol. Len Pearce won the scramble for the ball to earn the reward of a sovereign from the new captain. *Newbury Weekly News*

In the June stableford competition, Mrs Betty Boynton (34) recorded a score of net 53, which yielded a score of 49 points, reducing her handicap to 26.

*

It was agreed to purchase 50 bush poplar trees to be planted between 7th (5th) and 9th (7th) fairways.

*

Agreed the steward should buy 1 dozen dusters, 2 dozen tea towels, two fawn jackets, 1 dozen cups and saucers (and a partridge ...)

1969

It is known there are gravel deposits in various parts of the course, particularly to the left of the 3rd (12th) hole.
It was agreed to approach Messrs Airey Ltd to prospect the course for this material and determine possible value.

1970

Mr Rodford had been invited to attend the meeting, as a result of a complaint that he was seen playing towards the 12th (10th) green, when that hole was out of play, and also on the point that he had been late for the winter competitions on more than one occasion. He admitted playing several shots along the 13th, in reverse, he did not consider this in terms of practice, which is forbidden.

*

Since the new floor had been installed in the dining room, there had been accidents with people tilting their chairs backwards, and the chairs shooting from under them. Ferrules to be fitted.

1971

The captain was asked to speak to the steward to request a general improvement in familiarity, clearing the bar, over-charging, and drinking.

*

"The surprise of the opening round was the marathon defeat of Kent girl Jennifer Smith and her mother Dorothy, at the 21st hole, by the cheerful, happy-go-lucky partnership of Maureen Key and Janette Jolly of Newbury & Crookham, who were put out in the quarter finals.". (*Daily Mail* foursomes)

1972

The committee considered a note written in the suggestions book by Mr B.E.D. Cooper, who was present. They decided that, as it was more a complaint than a suggestion, the correct procedure should be for Mr Cooper to write a letter to the secretary for consideration by the committee.

*

Mr Hughes asked if the committee agreed to him charging fees as follows:
        Lessons, 1/2 hour, 75p. Playing fee per round, £1.50.
Agreed.

The committee thanked Mr R. Wilkinson for the generous gift of a large committee table.

1973

Letter from Mr Henderson – subject to shooting on course from a vehicle. The committee did not consider that this constituted a danger to life so long as it took place at night.

*

Bunkered at the 19th

Newbury & Crookham Golf Club have been without a bar for several weeks. The 10 year registration certificate had lapsed and the premises had ceased to be licensed. Magistrates Chairman Mr R.J. Huckle said "It might be an idea to tie a knot in your handkerchief". *(Newbury Weekly News)*

1974

The committee table has been de-wormed.

*

Permission was requested by Father Leonard of Douai Abbey for monks to play at a discount. Refused, but membership offered without joining fee as the Abbey held four debentures.

1975

Mr B.E.D. Cooper suggested that Frank Barton might consider attending an evening study course on "parks and greens maintenance". (Frank Barton had been greenkeeper since 1946).

*

The ladies section reported to the committee that they could not find space for the solarium that had been offered to the club.
There was a suggestion that it could be placed at the end of the committee room.

*

The tent loaned by Mr A.D. Seward's son-in-law for use at the 10th (8th) has been stolen.
Mr Ball suggested the club should purchase a replacement at the next off-peak sales period. Mr Seward believed that his son-in-law would prefer cash.

1976

Pellows Cup. A problem had arisen as two players had been seen practising on the 13th green. It was agreed that the intention of the committee was that men could play a round in the morning and this condition was not intended to include practice.

*

Urinal installation to be supervised by the secretary.

It was hoped that the house committee would look at the stools in the men's bar and have these suitably dealt with.

1977

A two-year-old horse called Willygo, scheduled to run in the first race on Saturday, threw his rider and went. He headed for the golf course and caused the Captain's Day competition to be temporarily abandoned as members pursued the runaway and cornered him near the 1st green. He was disqualified on both courses.

1978

Newbury & Crookham beat Goring & Streatley in a junior league match. John Miller, nephew of Geoff, won his match, 16 holes up.

1981

It was suggested that card schools be allowed to play in the committee room at a charge of £1.00 per school.

*

The Royal Wedding. The committee were undecided whether they should have a starting sheet.

*

After some discussion it was agreed that "warming drinks" be made available at the hut on special occasions.

*

There was a three-way play-off for the salver between Mrs Judith Sturgess, Mrs Sheila Hamilton and Mrs N Holford. This was an 18 hole medal play-off, and on being asked to produce their cards, they said they had thrown them away. All three were disqualified.

1984

Karen Davies was recently named "Pepsi Athlete of the Week" at the University of Florida where she is studying.

1988

Jack Hughes, speaking at his 80th birthday party about the course: "There are better and worse courses – but there is nothing quite like it, and I never tired of playing it." About the members: "They looked after me as a boy, and they still look after me now, that's why I never left".

The Roll of Honour

Albert Sancton Blyth Tull filled his fathers shoes in many walks of life: as Lord of the Manor of Crookham, High Sheriff of Berkshire, member of the county council, chairman of the Newbury county bench and rural district council, and, more relevantly, president of Crookham, Newbury District, and Newbury & Crookham Golf Clubs, a unique treble. He was president of Crookham 1912 to 1940, Newbury District 1944 to 1945, and Newbury & Crookham 1946 to 1952.

"Bertie" Tull was a golfer whereas his father was not. He enjoyed club life and won club trophies. In 1951 he was forced to retire from golf, and from office, through ill health. He died in 1954 aged 69.

E.H. (Harold) Bance, of Ball Hill, Newbury became president in 1952, after A.S.B. Tull had seen through the purchase of the course and the formation of the limited company. He was an ideal senior statesman, able to steer the club into the new era of self-ownership, which he did until 1963.

He first appears in competition reports for 1926, and joined the committee in 1930, becoming captain in 1935. His lowest handicap was eight.

He succeeded his father in the family building company, which was eventually taken over by his son Robert (captain 1954).

Robert A. (Bob) Bance had a distinguished war record being awarded the DFC in 1943, following attacks on targets in Holland, Belgium and France in conditions of extreme danger.

Sam Widdicombe (1889-1968) was club president in 1963-68. He began a legal career in Taunton, where after four years in a solicitor's office he entered the town clerk's department. He succeeded W.R. Pettifer as Newbury town clerk in 1922, retiring in 1949.

He was elected captain of Newbury District in 1938 and remained in office until 1945, steering the club through the war years.

A keen player and tireless worker, he was a leading negotiator during the purchase of the course. He and his wife were made life presidents of the club, an honour never previously bestowed.

He was president of Berkshire Bowling Association in 1964, the first member of Newbury Bowls Club to be so honoured. He was also a Berkshire captain, and Newbury Bowls Club President.

He played soccer for Taunton, and was a strong tennis player.

His daughters, Mrs Ruth Ball and Mrs Rachael Bance, both married prominent club members.

F.N. (Freddy) Ball President 1968–1975, was born in Newbury in 1912. He was the son of the headmaster of the Boys Secondary School (next to Black Boys Bridge, Newbury and recently demolished). His father was severely injured when the school was bombed during the last war.

He attended St Bartholomew's Grammar School, from which he joined the Newbury firm of solicitors, Charles Lucas & Marshall, of which the late club golfer, Angus Marshall, was senior partner.

During the war he served in the Royal Artillery, firstly in Coastal Command, and later in intelligence in the Far East. He left the service as a captain.

In 1941 he married Ruth, daughter of town clerk, and former president of Newbury & Crookham, Mr Sam Widdicombe.

Ball first appears in Newbury District records in 1927 (15 years old). He was Newbury & Crookham captain in 1949 and 1955, and followed his father-in-law as president. He was one of the club's best golfers, his lowest handicap being two, and a tireless worker for the club. He was also a leading figure in the negotiations and fund-raising prior to the purchase of the golf course, which ensured the future of the club. His generosity to the club was mostly anonymous, but two of the trophies bear his name, with that of his wife: the Family Foursomes (1962) and the Centenary Salver (1973).

Ruth Ball, lady captain in 1967, still frequently attends club functions.

Rex Hepburn, Peter Boynton and Freddie Ball, club presidents covering the years from 1968 to 1991

Peter Boynton was born at Whitby, on the east coast of Yorkshire in 1922. Ten years later he, and four others, constituted Whitby's first junior golf section. All were sons of members. He was eight handicap in 1939, when he joined the RAF. After the war he attended college, following which, in 1948, he took a position with an optician in Reading and joined Reading golf club. After moving to Woolwich in 1952, for the next six years he played golf only by paying green fees.

It was George Blake who suggested he should become a country member at Newbury & Crookham which he did in 1958. (Blake built, and owns,

Bishopswood Golf Club, but still plays regularly at Newbury & Crookham, which he joined in 1957, and of which he was captain in 1961).

After setting up his own practice in Thatcham, Peter became a full member in 1962, with his wife Betty and son John. He was elected to the committee in 1964, captain in 1967 and was president in 1975-86. He was chairman of the 1973 centenary committee. They now live at Pewsey and are active members of Tidworth Golf Club.

Peter has the gift of having good ideas, which are usually inspired by a sentimental regard for the history and tradition of the club, and golf in general.

When he became captain in 1967, he introduced the "driving in" ceremony. As previously written he and Betty donated the Boynton Salvers, the popular foursomes bogey competition. He can also be considered the founder of the Reading and District Inter Club Foursomes League, which unites its seven member clubs so well.

The annual fixture between teams of club captains and lady captains, culminates with an evening meal to which are invited all surviving captains and their partners. Peter Boynton instigated the fixture, and conducts the evening with rare warmth. In recent years the number of captains attending has regularly exceeded 50.

Rex Hepburn was born in Oldham, Lancashire, in 1921, moving to Southport at the age of three, his home for the next 27 years, with the exception of the war years. He joined Hillside Golf Club at the age of 13. After war service in India and Burma he studied at London University, where he was awarded his purple for golf by the College of St Mark and St John in 1950.

He moved to teach in Sussex in 1951 and joined West Hove Golf Club, becoming a committee member, involved particularly with handicaps and competitions, a role he was later to fill at Newbury & Crookham for more than seven years.

In the early 1960s he was a finalist in the Sussex Amateur championship, and won the West Sussex Open Winter Foursomes at Pulborough and the Sussex Open Winter Foursomes at Seaford Golf Club, East Blatchington.

He came to Newbury in 1964 as the first headmaster at the new Turnpike School.

In 1971 he was appointed Chief Field Officer to the Schools Council, retiring in 1981.

He joined Newbury & Crookham in 1964, became a committee member in 1968, captain in 1971 and president in 1986-91. He was elected a life member in 1993.

He was secretary of Berkshire Captains in 1984-91 and their captain in 1988.

Following the Berks, Bucks and Oxon County Championship victory at Ganton in 1986, he was elected to the Berks, Bucks and Oxon Executive Committee, and has been Junior delegate to the EGU, and manager of Berks, Bucks and Oxon juniors since 1992.

Roy Key, was born in Brockley, South East London in 1931, where he met, and married Maureen.

He became a chartered accountant which, when enlisting for his National Service, directed him into the Royal Army Pay Corps.

He moved to Newbury in 1964 to join British Hoist and Crane Company at Compton, becoming managing director in 1970.

He, with Maureen, started golf at Newbury & Crookham in 1966, and held office in the 19-plus section, but his concern about the financial affairs of the club, led him to join the committee in 1972. He became treasurer in 1975, and captain in 1979.

Roy Key

His fears were immediately justified when, in 1975, the subscription of £55 fell short of requirements and a £5 levy was added.

Before he became treasurer, the club had no reserve fund and was living a hand to mouth existence. In his 16 years as treasurer he steered the club from its old-fashioned attitude into the modern era, where golf clubs are businesses and should be run as such.

Long before he relinquished the post of treasurer in 1991, the club had a substantial reserve, and a healthy balance sheet, with future contingencies anticipated and budgeted well in advance.

In 1991 he was elected president, and has continued to oversee the affairs of the club with a fatherly care.

Maureen Key, lady captain in 1976-77, has given many years of service to the ladies committee.

Their daughter Janice played as a junior and lady member, before becoming a wife and mother. Son Raymond, a junior member in the early 70s, is waiting to rejoin the club.

Jack Hughes was born in Mill Lane, Newbury in 1908 and was educated at Newbury Council School, where his only ambition was to be a professional footballer. At 15 he applied for a vacancy at the yet unopened Newbury District Golf Club, and became shop assistant to the professional F.S. Perkins, although up to that time he had never held a golf club. He recalls his early days vividly, serving in the shop and "being a dogsbody for everyone".

Naturally he was initiated into club making and repairing. In his first nine years at the club there were only wooden shafted clubs in use, which meant much reshafting, whipping, "leading" and other repairs.

Jack Hughes in conversation with Henry Cotton

After a year Perkins was replaced by George Riches, who was to be Jack's employer for the next seven years. It may be supposed that the professional in those days would have taken young Jack under his wing, taught him how to play golf – and how to teach it. Jack is proud to relate that he was never given a lesson, but learned by watching the good players, and practising for hours.

The first recognition of Jack as a mature golfer was in a *Newbury Weekly News* report in 1928, covering an assistants championship held at Henley, in which he came second.

He is mentioned for the first time in the club minute books in December 1929, when, in response to a petition signed by many members, it was agreed that Jack would be offered the position of professional following the anticipated departure of Riches.

In 1931 Jack began his professional career, which was entirely spent at Newbury, until his retirement in 1977.

He played in major tournaments before, and after, the war including visits to the Open Championship.

He played with, and befriended, most of the famous players of his era. As for many other sportsmen of the late 1930s, the war came at the wrong time for Jack, and vital years of tournament golf were lost. He spent five years in the Royal Artillery, seeing active service in France and Germany.

His visits to the Open Championship began at Hoylake in 1936 followed by Sandwich, 1938. When next able to enter, at St Andrews in 1946, Jack was 39. Vital years had been lost. Records are not complete, even at the Royal & Ancient, and Jack cannot recall which Opens he attended. However, he definitely entered at Hoylake (1947), Lytham (1952), Birkdale (1954) and St Andrews (1960).

Jack's most recent success was in 1984 at Stratford-on-Avon, where he won the PGA Seniors over 70s title.

He twice won the Berks, Bucks & Oxon Professional Championship, and was the first captain of the Berks, Bucks and Oxon Professional Golfers Alliance. He held the professional records for Crookham (64) and Newbury (63), the latter being equalled in 1988 by Mark Howell of Henley.

At a monthly committee meeting in November 1952, it was proposed, and agreed, that Jack Hughes be made an honorary member of the club for his "long, loyal and willing service to the club". Surprisingly, the requirements of the constitution were overlooked, and the proposal was not placed before the next Annual General Meeting in August 1953.

Jack has known every member since 1923 and can recall most of them, usually with an anecdote. He combines cordiality, good humour and respect in a way which exemplifies the demeanour of professionals of "the old school". When quoting conversations with the pioneers of the club, it is noticeable that Jack addressed them as "sir".

A summary of Jack's achievements is not sufficient to convey the warmth with which he is regarded by all club members. How many of today's golfers, when playing the 13th, look ahead to the bench behind the green and, if Jack is there, put in an extra effort, or add some extra style, to impress him? When they have completed the hole, badly or otherwise, Jack will praise or encourage in a way which conveys a particular interest in that player's result; and he does it with every player.

Jack's swing was his hallmark – there is seldom a reference to Jack without a reference to his elegant, uncomplicated swing, which was still admired until he was forced to stop playing in 1991.

He lives only a few yards from the bench by the 13th and 18th greens, and not much further from the clubhouse, which he visits regularly. He is eagerly welcomed and never short of company.

In 1973 Jack received the following letter:

Professional Golfers' Association
National Headquarters
The Kennington Oval
London SE11

25th January 1973

Dear Mr Hughes,

It is my pleasant duty to inform you that at their meeting earlier this week the Executive Committee decided unanimously that as a mark of recognition of your long service and membership of the Professional Golfers' Association, you should be invited to accept Honorary Associate Membership.

Yours sincerely,

J. Bywaters
Secretary

Frank Barton was born in Newbury in 1918 and attended Newbury Council School.

At the age of 16 he was employed by Jack Hughes as an assistant. In those days hickory clubs were still in use and Frank's job included fitting shafts to iron heads, whipping the clubs and gripping them. He also made wooden club-heads from the prepared wedges that were bought in, fitting shafts, rams-horn or brass sole plates, and lead weighting.

In the $3^1/_2$ years he worked with Jack, Frank saw the demise of hickory clubs and the dawning of the new steel shaft era. He recalls, when the shop was overloaded with hickory clubs, abandoned or part exchanged, Jack had ordered him to "get rid of them". Frank took them to the sheds, chopped off the heads, burned the shafts, and buried the heads in rabbit holes.

Their hiding place is to remain a secret.

Frank was showing great promise as a golfer when surprisingly, in 1938, he joined the RAF.

When asked why he gave up golf so suddenly, Frank explained: "Oh, I never wanted to be a golfer, I only wanted to be a greenkeeper – that was all I ever wanted".

He tells of lunch times at the club when Jack would go home, instructing Frank to hit practice balls. "As soon as he was gone" says Frank "I was off, over to the sheds to see if I could cut a green or drive a tractor".

Frank realised there was no opportunity for him on the green staff at Newbury District so he gave up and became a trainee mechanic in the RAF. With the war following, Frank was in the RAF until 1946 and, upon leaving, took the first available job.

Fortunately, he soon encountered Jimmy Whitlock, the greenkeeper at the newly amalgamated Newbury & Crookham Club, who insisted that Frank should join him by taking the vacant assistant greenkeeper's job, which he did.

Shortly after this, failing health led Jimmy Whitlock to retire and Frank was promoted to greenkeeper in September 1946, a job he held with distinction until his retirement in 1986.

The eight years Frank spent as a mechanic in the RAF were to prove of inestimable value to the golf club because he has personally serviced and repaired the equipment, saving the club considerable time and money.

Following his retirement in 1986, there were two presentations made to him, one a gift from the members, the other from the club. Frank followed each of these presentations with a speech.

His eloquence, sincerity and romantic regard for his golf course, made these most moving occasions. He described early misty mornings, when deer and foxes frequently crossed his path. He explained in amusing detail how he had created many of our gullies, mounds, hollows and general landmarks throughout his years on the course, much of the work being done with little help and primitive equipment.

Frank expressed gratitude that he had spent his working life doing a job he loved.

Frank and his wife Hilda

He worked at the club on a full time basis until 1994, attending to the machinery, working in and around his immaculate workshop, surrounded by relics and pictures of the past, willing always to share his knowledge and love for his course with anyone who cared to call.

David Harris, club professional, was born in Galashiels, Roxburghshire, and first played golf at Melrose Golf Club. He worked in a local bank but having attained a six handicap, decided that he was more inspired by golfing than banking, and took an appointment as assistant at Sonning in 1966, aged 19.

He moved several times, working at Henley, Huntercombe, West Hill and Flackwell Heath, where he spent five years before coming to Newbury in 1975, as assistant to Jack Hughes. There were specific terms that, upon Jack's imminent retirement, he was to become the club professional, which he did in 1977.

David won the Berks, Bucks and Oxon assistants championship in 1976, and the Berks, Bucks and Oxon professional championship in 1989. He was captain of the Berks, Bucks and Oxon professionals in 1985 and served as their representative on the Berks, Bucks and Oxon Alliance for ten years.

David Harris, extreme left, pictured with his former assistants (left to right) James Purton, Richard Howett, Gareth Williams and Adie Waters at the Newbury & Crookham Pro-Am 1994. All are club professionals in the Newbury area.

Newbury & Crookham is fortunate to have an experienced and dedicated professional whose enthusiasm for the game is as eager now as it was when he arrived.

His assistant professional is Lee Newman who arrived in 1993 from Calcot Golf Club.

Philip Greader, honorary secretary of the club from 1945 to 1965, was born at West Kington, Wiltshire in 1905. He was a member of Newbury Hockey Club and Newbury Squash Club (then situated in Pembroke Road). He also played for Wiltshire Moonrakers, an elite hockey team based at Marlborough.

He was the last "honorary" secretary, and, as indicated in contributions by Frank Barton, he had such an individual approach to the position that the title of "general manager" would have been more apt.

He did much towards the rebuilding of the course at the end of the war, at one time organising prisoners of war to work, at a penny an hour. He was captain in 1960 and died in 1968.

Mrs Dorothea (Dolly) Greader, lady captain in 1951 and 1961, lady president in 1974-80, still enjoys playing, but son Tim, captain in the Centenary Year, one of the many strong players of the 1960s and 1970s, now plays less competitive golf.

Anne Thomas, daughter of ex Crookham member Len Moore and his late wife Win, won her first club tournament, the junior handicap, in 1950, when she was 15 and her most recent in 1993.

To date she has won ten of the 23 club scratch championships held since 1972, plus once tying with Karen Davies, but losing the play off. She has won at least 55 trophies at Newbury & Crookham:

Priston	1951
Silver Handicap Salver	1984
Boynton Bogey	1992
Platt	1965
Scratch Championship	1972,73,76,77,78,84,85,88,89,92
Crookham Foursomes	1952,54,57
Centenary Plate	1991
Win Moore	1985
Stokes Salver	1951,52,53,55,61,62,63, 65,68,70,72
Douglas	1992
Boake	1993
Jean Cup	1954
Jean & Whiteley	1963,80,85
Junior Handicap	1950
Philbrick	1964,65,66,67,68,69,74,80,85,91,92
Gilroy	1950,51,73
Pellows	1980
Golfer of the Year	1985,91,92

The above career record has been put together despite her full time occupation.

She was Berkshire ladies captain in 1984 and lady captain at Newbury & Crookham in 1986. She was Berkshire county president in 1991-94.

Chris Ball born in 1944 was first mentioned in a golf report in 1957 and won his first club trophy, the junior handicap in 1958. Since then he has added another 58 club trophies, including a record eight club championships (the Dunn Trophy). He has been Master Golfer eight times. His best year was 1964, when he won seven titles and he is still a threat to the young hopefuls of the club, winning the Elkington (scratch knock-out),and the club foursomes in 1994.His full club record is:

Captain & Pro	1964,66,71,73,83,85
Fourball	1964,65,67,72,73,87,90,92
Elkington	1964,78,81,94
Fairhurst	1968,71
Kirby	1963,64,85
Junior Scratch	1962
Junior H'cap	1958

Foursomes	1964,66,69,72,73,90,93,94
Ronaldshay	1966,70,72,75,85
Family Foursomes	1983
Dunn Trophy	1964,65,68,69,70,71,76,78
Newbury & Crookham Bogey	1962
Portal	1971
Gilroy	1978,79
Masters	1964,65,66,70,71,72,73,85

In 1973 he became club captain, the youngest holder of the office, at 28. His lowest handicap was one, which he held for 18 years.

His record on behalf of the club has been exceptional, being a member of the club team on the four occasions it won the Berks, Bucks and Oxon club scratch foursomes, and the five occasions it has won the foursomes league.

His amateur career was to some extent restricted by necessary studies to follow his father's footsteps as a solicitor, but he played for Berks, Bucks and Oxon from 1964 to 1974 and was a member of the side that won the EGU championship at Saunton in 1969. He won the West of England Matchplay championships at Burnham & Berrow in 1970. He was non- playing captain of Berks, Bucks and Oxon Union of Golf Clubs in 1977-79.

Geoffrey Miller was born in 1944 and attended St Bartholomew's Grammar School. He, and others who shared the interest, joined Newbury &

Crookham and became pupils of Jack Hughes. Miller immediately stood out, being strong, but elegant, and was soon representing the club in what was a very productive era. He won the Dunn Trophy four times and, with Ball and Cronin, provided some memorable club championships in 1963-73.

He represented the Berks, Bucks and Oxon junior teams and made his debut for the first team in 1963.

In 1966 he won a golfing blue at Cambridge and won all his matches in the 22-7 defeat of Oxford. He played again in 1967 and maintained his 100 per cent record.

After leaving university, he moved to London and later to the West Country, where he now lives.

Peter Cronin, the youngest of the exciting trio of the 1960s, born in 1948, was a short, slightly-built left-hander who, despite being equal to the talents of Ball and Miller, could only win one club championship, in 1972.

The trio represented the club in the Berks, Bucks and Oxon Club Scratch Foursomes and brought home the trophy in 1969. In 1970, with Miller, and in 1972, with Greader, Cronin won the Berks, Bucks and Oxon Foursomes Championship.

Playing in the Dunn Trophy in 1968 he set a new course record of 63. His enjoyment of this was dimmed when he was overtaken by Ball in the second round, but Ball is quoted as saying that his victory would be soon forgotten, whereas Cronin's 63 would be remembered for years.

Cronin moved away from Newbury and no longer plays golf.

John Niven, born in Scotland in 1920, was a one handicap player at Ardeer Golf Club before volunteering for flying duties with the RAF in 1940. He was trained as a pilot, commissioned, and did three tours of operations on low level daylight attacks, plus later intruder operations on targets in occupied Europe. He was also heavily involved in the D-Day landings and was awarded the DFC.

After the war, when service commitments permitted, he played in the Amateur Championship, reaching the last 16 at Royal St Georges in 1948 and the fourth round at Royal Lytham (1955) and Formby (1957).

He was RAF champion in 1948. Playing with the professionals in the Northern Scottish Open in 1950, he finished 5th, and leading amateur. Whilst in Malaya during the Emergency, he won the Selangor Championship in 1953 and 1954 and the North Malayan Championship, also in 1954. In 1957 he won the Berks, Bucks and Oxon Championship.

He retired from the RAF in 1958 as a squadron leader, and joined Newbury & Crookham in 1964. In 1979 he won the club championship, The Dunn Trophy, repeating the win in 1989, when, at the age of 69, he became, and remains, its oldest winner. His first round score of 68 was one under his age.

In seniors golf he has won the Berks, Bucks and Oxon Championship four times, and won the Scottish Open Seniors in 1982. In the British Seniors Championship he won the over-65 age group in 1989, and the English over 70 group in 1991.

He was captain of the RAF golf team from 1956 to 1958, captain of the Berks, Bucks and Oxon county side and, later, president of the union.

John's wife Bobs also plays at Newbury and together they won the prestigious Fleming Foursomes, which is also open to professionals, at Sunningdale Ladies Golf Club in 1988-89.

John is a member of the Royal and Ancient and with Bobs, sons Alastair and David, and daughter Emma, are members of the Royal Cinque Ports G.C. at Deal.

David Niven was club junior champion (1973), won the Berks, Bucks and Oxon Junior Championship at the age of 16, and was an England Boys' trialist. He has been club champion seven times, between 1974 and 1986. He was a regular member of the triple counties team, and was in the Berks, Bucks and Oxon side that won the English County Championship in 1983, the team being captained by father John Niven. In open competition he won the Frilford Gold Medal (1982) and the Prince of Wales Challenge at Deal (1984).

Chris Ball presenting the Dunn Trophy to David Niven, 1974

In the English Championship, at his first attempt he reached the last 16, and later had two notable failures, losing to Michael Bonallack at the 20th, and Peter McEvoy by one hole.

In the late 1980s he took up the triathalon and competed in the Iron Man in Hawaii. In 1993 he was selected for the British over 35s team for the World Championships in Nice.

In 1995 John and David Niven won the Father & Sons competition at West Hill, playing seven rounds in four days.

Bert How, born in 1920, was a junior member of Flackwell Heath from 1936.

He joined the Fleet Air Arm in 1939 and spent 22 years in the service, seeing action in the Second World War and the Korean War.

He was the first unranked player to represent the Navy, which he did on more than 50 occasions.

For ten years of his prime Bert was a one handicap player, and has held three amateur course records, at Liphook, Hayling Island and Henbury, being selected for Hampshire whilst a member of Liphook.

He has been a member of 27 clubs and has held the club championship at "15 or 16" of them. He joined Newbury & Crookham in 1969, and won the club championship in 1977. Bert considers his best performances were when winning the Moray Open and, more recently, the South West Counties Seniors Championship. He still plays regularly at Newbury off a handicap of 11.

Stephanie Jane Jolly, with her older sister Sarah, joined Newbury & Crookham in 1971, at the age of 11. Her mother Janette, lady captain in 1995, and father, John, were already members, both taking up the game in the early 1960s.

Stephanie (known more generally as "Steph") achieved almost immediate success, winning the Junior Handicap Cup with 75-27=48.

Jack Hughes, her coach and mentor, considers that Stephanie represents his greatest success. At the age of 12 she entered the English Girls Championship and in 1974 won the club scratch championship, at 14 the youngest to do so.

At the age of 15 she won the Berkshire Junior Championship, closely followed by the Berkshire Ladies Championship, in which she defeated Pam Cardy in the final at the Berkshire Golf Club. Later in 1975 she also won the Tegner Trophy at Temple, another county 36 hole scratch event. She was selected to represent England Girls in the 1975 home international series for the Stroyan Cup, played at Henbury. England retained the trophy, Stephanie winning her three matches. In the same year she reached the semi final of the British Girls Championship and made her debut in the British and English Ladies Championships.

In 1976 she again represented England in the Stroyan Cup, winning two matches, and halving one. She reached the semi-final of the English Girls Championship, played at Moseley, losing at the last hole.

In a match promoted by the ELGA, Stephanie played professional Vivienne Saunders at Newbury in 1976, losing on the 18th. In the same year she was selected to represent England in the home internationals at Troon and was a reserve for the British Curtis Cup team.

In 1977 she again represented England in the Stroyan Cup, winning two matches and losing one, followed by three wins in 1978, giving her a cup record of: played 12, won 10, lost one and halved one. She also played in a two girl England team in an international tournament, "The 13th Challenge Hassan II" at Royal Golf Dar-es-Salaam, Rabat. The team finished runners-up to France, Stephanie having third best individual score. She received her trophy, a silver apple, from King Hassan II. The previous week she played in the Spanish championships, and, within the same month, entered the French Open at St Cloud, near Paris.

In 1978 she represented England in the 11th European U23 Team Championship, held at Is Molas Golf Club, Sardinia, and was invited to play in the Colgate European LPGA Championship at Sunningdale.

One of her last appearances as an amateur was at the South Eastern Girls Championship held at Newbury. She was paired with Sue Bamford in the first round and trailed her by five shots. In the afternoon she scored a course record 67 to win by one shot.

Stephanie became a professional in October 1978, with three other colleagues. The most significant sponsor was Carlsberg, who agreed to support a series of 12 events to be staged throughout the country. The prize money was not enough to meet their expenses, but they were at least on their way.

The original group, who were founders of the Women's Professional Golfers' Association, were awarded life membership. Her professional career was halted when, in 1982, she married Ewen Murray, a tournament professional, who later became a TV golf commentator. "Two of a kind" in one family did not work and Stephanie took to the road with her husband around the European circuit.

Stephanie later re-married and, with husband Mark, a New Zealander, moved to Dubai, where she resumed her golfing interest, joining the management team setting up the Dubai Creek and Yacht Club. On completion she moved to the Emirates Golf Club, becoming its lady professional, and shop manager.

Stephanie moved to New Zealand in 1993 and lives in Gisborne. She and Mark now have a son, and in memory of her "Uncle Jack", they have named him Samuel John.

David Rosier joined the club in 1975 at the age of 13. By 1977 his handicap was nine, by 1978, four, and by 1979, three.

Apart from his progress on the domestic scene, 1979 was a progressive and productive year. He played in the Carris Trophy at Moor Park, now known as the English Boys Amateur Open Championship. In the opening round on the West Course, he scored 6 on the par 3 2nd hole and struggled to finish only six over par. In the second round, on the High Course, he was one over par, ending the day in 11th place. On the second day he played two rounds on the High Course in level par, to finish runner-up, four shots behind the winner D. Hammond. As a result of this he was selected to travel as first reserve for the England Boys team in their annual international against Scotland, at Barassie, but was unfortunately not used. As England boys play only one international match each year, there was no second chance.

His major successes were winning the Frilford Gold Medal in 1979, and the West of England Matchplay Championship in 1987. He played for ten years at the top level of amateur golf, representing the club and the triple counties with distinction. He is now only a social member at Newbury & Crookham and, although holding a country membership at Burnham & Berrow, has virtually retired from the game.

David Rosier with the West of England matchplay Championship cup, 1987

Karen Davies arrived at Newbury & Crookham in 1979 and attended St Bartholomew's School. Previously a member of Wrexham Golf Club, she was already a well-groomed golfer and in 1980, aged 15, she won the Denbighshire Ladies County Championship and the Welsh Girls Championship, repeating the latter success in 1982.

At Newbury & Crookham she won the club scratch championship in 1981 and 1983.

She represented Wales in the European Ladies Junior team championships at

Wentworth in 1981 and became a full international in the same year.

In 1984 she took up a four year golf scholarship at the University of Florida, in Gainsville, reading history for her degree.

In the semi-final of the British Women's Open Championship in 1985, she lost to the eventual winner Lillian Behan. She lost again in the 1987 semi final. Her handicap at this time was plus five, the lowest ladies handicap ever recorded.

The pinnacle of her amateur career came in the Curtis Cup matches of 1986 and 1988, both won by Great Britain, and in which Karen won all four of her foursomes matches, and halved two and lost one of her singles.

Her amateur record was:

for Wales:	Home Internationals 1981,82,83
	European Ladies Team Championships 1987
for Great Britain:	Curtis Cup 1986,88
	Vagliano Trophy 1987
	Commonwealth International 1987

Following four successful years at university, during which time she won nine tournaments, she turned professional in 1988. In her first year she played in 15 tournaments, her best finish being joint 6th. Her earnings were £10,557 and she finished 41st in the rankings. She has since maintained a full and rewarding career, qualifying for the LPGA tour in 1991 and 1992. In 1993-94 she played most of her golf in Europe, returning to America for the Future's Tour, winning the Central Florida Challenge in November 1994. Early in 1995 she had five top 20 finishes on the Asian Tour, and came back to Europe in the summer on the Women's Professional Golf European Tour, now called the American Express Tour.

Scott Watson was born in 1966 in Newbury. He started golf at Tylney Park at the age of 12. His mentor was John Niven, who encouraged him to join Newbury & Crookham, where he became junior champion in 1982.

In 1984 he reached the quarter finals of the British Boys Championship. He later joined North Hants Golf Club and became a Hampshire county player.

He turned professional in 1988 when he joined Stoneham Golf Club, and won his first pro-am, at Tylney Park.

He qualified for his European Tour Card in 1993 after several attempts, and retained it in 1994.

In 1995 former member Richard Fortmuller became professional at Deanwood Park and Nigel Hart, junior champion at Newbury & Crookham, joined Drayton Golf Club as assistant professional. Julian Sandys, club champion in 1993 and 1994 became assistant professional at Henley Golf Club.

Today's People

A golf club is the sum of many parts: its employees, its members, its course, its politicians, and its history.

Kevin Beardsley and his wife Shirley, arrived in 1992, since when they have considerably developed the standard of the dining and social facilities.

Kevin Beardsley,
Steven Griffiths, Lee Newman,
David Harris, Shirley Beardsley,
June Hearsey, Amanda Fisher

Kevin Tilly, Ross Wilson, Thomas
Stantiford, Richard Dalmas,
Lewis Warwick

1995 Juniors (back to front and
left to right)

David Hall (J.O.), Oliver Smyth,
Oliver Wilde, Martin Davey,
June Hearsey (Sec),
Graham Purton (Capt),
Nicholas Chappel,
Eddie Richardson, Neil Terry,
Toby Cummins, Lucy Passey,
Darren Hill, William Forbes

With cups: Barry Newman,
Neil Halls

Greenkeeper Steven Griffiths succeeded David Heads in 1990, and immediately encountered problems with the condition of the greens. There was no blame attached to him, and since then he has provided playing conditions of a very high standard.

The club secretary, June Hearsey completed 25 years at Newbury & Crookham in October 1995. She is a secretary of rare quality and is held in high esteem by other secretaries in the county. Originally assistant to Ron Church, she took over as club secretary in 1989. In the ensuing years she has seen all office procedures transferred to computers. In this she has, since 1992, been assisted by Amanda Fisher, who, apart from being a secretary, has responsibility for the club's accounting system.

Of today's young players, probably Nick Woodage shows most promise. Down to one handicap as a result of some under par scores early in 1995, he was then too late to enter national events for that year, but is a player to follow in the near future. Tim Butler, who returns to Newbury from his American college each summer, is a prodigious player for whom there must surely be an exciting future.

Younger still, there are several players with potential, and much credit is due to David Harris and Gareth Williams. Eddie Richardson, Andrew Baylis, Barry Newman, Ashley and Oliver Wilde, Toby Cummins, and our only girl, Lucy Passey. From these names there may emerge a champion, but that is in the future ...

The members, and especially their elected officers, are the custodians of an historic club with a romantic history. They are shareholders in more ways than one. Perhaps this book will serve as a reminder of how things were before they arrived, that they may have an increased respect for the club, and the course, to moderate their ambitions.

The following extract from the foreword to *The History of Formby Golf Club*, provides a fitting final paragraph:

> What is more important is that this book makes us realise that each succeeding generation of members have left things better for their successors. This surely is the essence of a great golf club.

Appendix

PRESIDENTS

Newbury District

1923-41	Lord Ronaldshay (The Marquis of Zetland)
1942-44	Col. J. Fairhurst
1944-45	A.S.B. Tull

Newbury & Crookham

1946-52	A.S.B. Tull
1952-63	E.H. Bance
1963-68	S. Widdicombe
1968-75	F.N. Ball
1975-86	P. Boynton
1986-91	R. Hepburn
1991-96	R. Key

LADY PRESIDENTS

Newbury District

1923-37	Mrs Lloyd H. Baxendale
1938-39	Mrs Bramwell Davis

Newbury & Crookham

1947-56	Mrs Austin Dickson
1956-61	Lady des Veoux
1961-63	Mrs H.I. Taylor
1963-69	Mrs K. Graham
1969-74	Mrs V.E. Clippendale
1974-81	Mrs D. Greader
1981-82	Mrs W. Moore
1983-87	Mrs F. Fox
1987-93	Mrs E. Southern
1993	Mrs C. Longden

CAPTAINS

Newbury District

1923-26	J.A. Fairhurst	1934	N.W. Tredinnick	1937	J.S. Rutherford
1927-30	C.E. Gilroy	1935	E.H. Bance	1938-45	S. Widdicombe
1931-33	W.K.T. Hope	1936	A.M. Collard		

Newbury & Crookham

1946	E.T. Povey	1963	J. Reynolds	1981	P.G. Mead
1947	C. de V. Buckingham	1964	P.E. Risby	1982	F.F. Fisher
1948	F.M. Barton	1965	J.E.B. Dyson	1983	B.A. Tims
1949	F.N. Ball	1966	D.H.P. Henderson	1984	J.A. Hamilton
1950	T.H. Evans	1967	A.P. Boynton	1985	G.R. Davies
1951	H.I. Taylor	1968	J.G. Miller	1986	R.J. Heitzman
1952	K. Huxtable	1969	M.G. Simmons	1987	J.W. Calkin
1953	W.F. Perry	1970	F.C. Goodenough	1988	J.A. Mackay
1954	R.A. Bance	1971	R. Hepburn	1989	R.I. Bates
1955	F.N. Ball	1972	T.P. Greader	1990	G.G. Woodage
1956	J. Marshall	1973	C.J. Ball	1991	B.A. Teece
1957	J.D. Knowles	1974	A.D. Seward	1992	C.S. Arnold
1958	F.L. Shergold	1975	R.A. Wilkinson	1993	G.G. Woodage
1959	W.J. Barlow	1976-77	H.A. Martin	1994	A.P. Butler
1960	P.H. Greader	1978	I. Dent	1995	G. Purton
1961	G.T. Blake	1979	R.J. Key		
1962	E. Howard	1980	B.A. Haskell		

LADY CAPTAINS

Newbury District

1923	Mrs. Cosmo-Douglas	1930-31	Mrs Urling	1935-40	Miss Stokes
1924-27	Miss Kitkat	1932	Mrs Austin Dickson		
1927-30	Mrs Austin Dickson	1933-35	Mrs Stow		

Newbury & Crookham

1940-46	Mrs Austin Dickson	1964	Mrs C.M. Longdon	1981	Mrs C.M. Longden
1947	Mrs L. Moore	1965	Mrs L. Southern	1982	Mrs E.M Mackay
1948-49	Mrs H.I. Taylor	1966	Mrs J.B. Dyson	1983	Mrs G.R. Bowness
1950	Miss M.K. Heather	1967	Mrs F.N. Ball	1984	Mrs A.D. Brown
1951	Mrs P.H. Greader	1968	Mrs M. Lloyd	1985	Mrs V. Wilshire
1952	Mrs T.H.G. Bostock	1969	Mrs E.D. Evans	1986	Mr A. Thomas
1953	Mrs K. Huxtable	1970	Mrs H. Howard	1987	Mrs. J. Reid
1954-55	Mrs D. Grahame	1971	Mrs R.G. Freemantle	1988	Mrs J. Forster
1956	Mrs W.C. Clippingdale	1972	Mrs K.N. Worthington	1989	Mrs M.J. Rodgers
1957	Mrs E.R. Bostock	1973	Mrs R. Pierce-Williams	1990	Mrs B.F. Rolfe
1958	Miss E.M. Aird	1974	Mrs J.C. McNiece	1991	Mrs J. Birch
1959	Mrs H. Taylor	1975	Mrs P.D. Clarke	1992	Mrs D.F. Gunnersen
1960	Miss M.K. Heather	1976-77	Mrs R.J. Key	1993	Mr S.H. Elvey
1961	Mrs P.H. Greader	1978	Mrs S.J. Hamilton	1994	Mrs E.A. Dunks
1962	Mrs S. Baker	1979	Mrs A.H. Brown	1995	Mrs J. Jolly
1963	Mrs.H.F. Fox	1980	Mrs F.E. Dance		

SECRETARIES

Newbury District

1923	Col. Stanton & Cmdr R.B. England	1942-44	L.E. Yeomans
1924-26	Cmdr England	1945	P.H. Greader
1927-41	C.W. Bloxham		

Newbury & Crookham

1946-64	P.H. Greader	1973-76	R.J. Williams (first full time)
1965-68	C.S. Barron (first paid, part time)	1976-89	R. Church
1969-71	S.M. Wilson (part time)	1989	Mrs J. Hearsey
1972-73	G. Adams (part time)		

HON. TREASURERS

Newbury District

1923-41	J. Greenshields	1942-45	R. Kerr

Newbury & Crookham

1946-51	R. Kerr	1968-74	D. Abbott
1952-61	E.C. Deacon	1975-91	R. Key
1962-66	E.W. Blackburn	1992-95	G. Dunks
1966-67	B. Fielding	1995-	S. Creffield

PROFESSIONALS

Newbury District

1922-24	F.S. Perkins
1924-31	G. Riches
1931-39	J. Hughes

Newbury & Crookham

1946-77	J. Hughes
1977-	D. Harris

GREENKEEPERS

Newbury District

1923	W. Field
1924-32	A. Kirkpatrick
1933-45	J. Whitlock

Newbury & Crookham

1946	J. Whitlock
1946-87	F. Barton
1987-90	D. Head
1990	S. Griffiths

The Club Championship - The Dunn Trophy

Best gross score in Fairhurst Cup

1949	J. Casserley 79+76=155
	(after play-off with L. Moore)
1950	L. Moore
1951	L. Moore
1952	J. Whiting 78+73=151
1953	Sgt R. Rhymar 75+78=153
	(USA)
1954	C.V. Leibscher 76+73=149
	(USA)
1955	C.V. Leibscher 71+76=147
1956	F.N. Ball
1957	L.J. Stradling 77+78=155
1958	L.J. Stradling 75+73=148
1959	L.J. Stradling 85+76=161
1960	F.N. Ball
1961	R.J.K. Horn
1962	L.J. Stradling = 149
1963	G.W. Miller 73+81=154
1964	C.J. Ball 77+76=153

Separated from Fairhurst Cup

1965	C.J. Ball 73+71=144
1966	G.W. Miller 71+73=144
1967	G.W. Miller 69+69=138
1968	C.J. Ball 68+72=140
1969	C.J. Ball 68+72=140
1970	C.J. Ball* 65+69=134
1971	C.J. Ball 71+73=144

1972	P.T. Cronin 70+72=142
1973	G.W. Miller 69+70=139
1974	D.H. Niven 74+71=145
1975	T.P. Greader 69+70=139
1976	C.J. Ball 71+67=138
1977	A.J. How 67+75=142
1978	C.J. Ball 73+72=145
1979	J. Niven 70+73=143
1980	D.H. Niven 71+71=142
1981	D.H. Niven 72+69=141
1982	D.H. Niven 70+71=141
1983	D.P. Rosier 68+69=137
	Par 67 SSS 68
1984	D.H. Niven 71+67=138
	Par 68 SSS 68
1985	D.H. Niven 75+73=148
	(36-hole play-off with L. Watkins)
1986	D.H. Niven 71+68=139
1987	D.P. Rosier 66+72=138
1988	R.J. Claridge 71+73=144
1989	J. Niven 68+74=142
1990	T.J. Butler 74+73=147
	(4-hole play-off with D. Rosier)
1991	I. Briggs 72+72=144
1992	T.J. Butler 74+71=145
1993	J.G. Sandys 64+71=137
1994	J.G. Sandys 72+69=141
1995	B. Davies 67+71=138

* Lowest score

Youngest winner: 1990 T.J. Butler, 16 years 4 months

Oldest winner: 1989 J. Niven, 69 years.

Newbury & Crookham Bogey

(Originally (1874) the Crookham Handicap Challenge Cup, previous winners listed in the Crookham section)

1947	T.H. Evans	1963	G.W. Miller	1979	R.O. Drummond
1948	R. Morrison	1964	T. Pinnock	1980	G.T. Blake
1949	W.J. Barlow	1965	I.M. Dyke	1981	J. Green
1950	R.A. Bance	1966	G.T. Blake	1982	C.A. Waldeck
1951	F.N. Ball	1967	L. Moore	1983	B.A. Tims
1952	A.J. Swanson	1968	G. Sinclair-Jones	1984	R.G. Robson
1953	J. Whiting*	1969	L. Watkins	1985	P. Haine
1954	J. Keates	1970	A. How	1986	A.J. Axford
1955	F.A.H. Keates	1971	P.E. Risby	1987	G.D. Rowlands
1956	W.E. Jenkins	1972	C.J. Hall	1988	G. Gunnersen
1957	H.J. Barlow	1973	A. Panting	1989	B.A. Teece
1958	A.E. Pearce	1974	A.R. Willock	1990	B.W. Bradshaw
1959	L. Moore*	1975	B. Bradshaw	1991	D. Picton
1960	R.J. Horn	1976	N. Beeler	1992	H. Dobson
1961	J.E.B. Dyson	1977	R.C. Miles	1993	T.A. Furr
1962	C.J. Ball	1978	B.L. Sturgess	1994	T. Paynter
				1995	N.G. Woodage

* Double winners at Crookham and Newbury.

Newbury & Crookham Medal Cup

(Formerly the Crookham Open Challenge Cup)

1947	J. Whiting	1963	P.E. Risby	1979	D.N.J. Elliott
1948	A.R.G. Rodford	1964	T. Pinnock	1980	M. Gunnersen
1949	F.M. Barton	1965	M. Simmons	1981	M. Bradford
1950	R.A. Bance	1966	P.T. Cronin	1982	R.C. Miles
1951	K. Huxtable	1967	F.E. Dance	1983	A.J. Aylett
1952	F.N. Ball	1968	E. Howard	1984	J.D. Burns
1953	J.P. Hayley	1969	M.J.D. Powell	1985	J.C. Lovette (USA)
1954	J. Griffin	1970	A.C. Smith	1986	T.D. Johnson
1955	F.L. Shergold	1971	R. Bishop	1987	A.P. Butler
1956	A.J. Molner (USA)	1972	J. Niven	1988	J.A. Mackay
1957	P.H. Greader	1973	A.J. Panting	1989	N.G. Woodage
1958	J.A. Thistlewood	1974	J.E. Cripps	1990	L.A. Harris
1959	G. Bowden	1975	M.R. Drake	1991	J. Clor (USA)
1960	T.P.N. Greader	1976	R.J. Marchant	1992	K. Dunks
1961	F.N. Ball	1977	A. Shirtliff	1993	R. Foulkes
1962	R. Black	1978	B.F. Fox	1994	R. Belfield
				1995	T. Paynter

The Captain's Cup

(Changed to the Fairhurst Cup in 1932)

1924	W.K.T. Hope		1962	D. Fyffe
1925	N.W. Tredinnick		1963	G.W. Miller
1926	J.B. Lee		1964	L. Moore
1927	F.J. Kirby		1965	M.J. Waterman
1928	N.W. Tredinnick		1966	L.M. Dyke
1929	J.B. Lee		1967	P.T. Cronin
1930	W.K.T. Hope		1968	C.J. Ball
1931	N.W. Tredinnick		1969	B. Williams
	(won outright)		1970	R. Black

Fairhurst Cup

			1971	C.J. Ball
1932	R.C.R. Clark		1972	T.P. Greader
1933	N.W. Tredinnick		1973	I.P.J. Gibbs
1934	S. Widdicombe		1974	M. Shaw
1935	W.K.T. Hope		1975	D. Elliott
				(youngest winner at 16)
1936	H.C. Smith		1976	B. Sturgess
1937	W.K.T. Hope		1977	J.G. Miller
1938	E. Yarwood		1978	M.J. Waterman
1939	J.S. Rutherford		1979	R. Garner
1946	W.K.T. Hope		1980	E.D.G. Long
1947	L. Moore		1981	G.G. Woodage
1948	W.C. Clippingdale		1982	R. Williams
1949	P.H. Greader		1983	R.J. Carter
1950	R.A. Bânce		1984	J. Purton
1951	R. Morrison		1985	D.W. Strubble* (USA)
1952	P.J. Chaplin		1986	K. Dunks
1953	R. Rhymar (USA)		1987	G.D. Rowlands
1954	C.V. Liebscher (USA)		1988	M.M. Howard
1955	J.P.J. Riopel (USA)		1989	L.A. Harris
1956	D.L. Gibbons		1990	M.J. Hutchins
1957	A.J. Huckle		1991	S. Hunt
1958	T.P. Greader		1992	T.J. Butler
1959	P.H. Greader		1993	K.L. Lawson
1960	T.P. Greader		1994	K.L. Lawson
1961	G. Holloway		1995	T.J. Riordan

* Lowest score 64+60=124 off 18 handicap

Ronaldshay Cup

1925	A. Saunderson	1953	F.N. Ball	1975	A. How
1926	A. Saunderson	1954	L. Moore	1976	R.J. Bishop
1927	M.O. Wells	1955	D.J. Hopson	1977	P. Sievers
1928	H.D. Floyd	1956	A.J. Molnar	1978	R.J. Bishop
1929	J.T. Louch	1957	N. Gillman	1979	C.J. Ball
1930	A. Marshall	1958	R. Goerdt	1980	A.S. Wood
1931	F.N. Ball	1959	T.P. Greader	1981	J. Niven
1932	F.N. Ball	1960	C.L. Garry	1982	P.T. Cronin
1933	J.B. Lee	1961	J.E.B. Dyson	1983	P.F. Sievers
1934	F.N. Ball	1962	G.T. Blake	1984	A.S. Wood
1935	J.S. Rutherford	1963	A.P. Boynton	1985	C.J. Ball
1936	E.T. Povey	1964	A.P. Boynton	1986	J. Niven
1937	W.K.T. Hope	1965	H.D. Loader	1987	R.J. Claridge
1938	J.S. Rutherford	1966	C.J. Ball	1988	G.R. Gee
1939	E.T. Povey	1967	R.H. Purdue	1989	A.J. Axford
1946	L. Moore	1968	J. Niven	1990	R. Cox
1947	L. Moore	1969	I.M. Dyke	1991	K. Dunks
1948	J.W. Casserley	1970	C.J. Ball	1992	N. Woodage
1949	J.R. Moore	1971	R. Black	1993	B. Davies
1950	R. Tull	1972	C.J. Ball	1994	I. Briggs
1951	W.C. Clippingdale	1973	R.A. Bance	1995	N.G. Woodage
1952	M. Lewis	1974	P.E. Risby		

Portal Cup

Presented in 1904 by E.R. Portal to Hungerford Golf Club where it was played for as the Challenge Cup.

The winners at Hungerford, whose names are engraved on the cup, are:

May 1904	J. McKerlie	December 1911	W. Dickson MD
December 1904	John Russell	May 1912	J.C. Adnams
June 1905	F.W. Church	December 1912	J.C. Adnams
December 1905	J. McKerlie	May 1913	W.S. Butler
June 1906	W.H. Belcher	December 1913	H.G. Wigglesworth
December 1906	J. McKerlie	June 1914	D. Cookson
May 1907	J. Russell	December 1920	A.R. Peart
December 1907	J. Russell	March 1921	I. Marjorie Platt
June 1908	J. Russell	November 1921	A.R. Peart
December 1908	J. Russell	December 1922	T.C. Starkey-Smith
May 1909	A.R. Peart	July 1923	H.J. Broadbent
December 1909	F.W. Peart	December 1923	A.R. Peart
May 1910	J. Russell	April 1924	W.H. Taylor
December 1910	J. Russell	December 1924	A.R. Peart
June 1911	W.S. Butler	June 1925	E.R. Portal

Portal Cup continued

After the closure of Hungerford, presented to Newbury District. Played as a flag competition.

1926	A. Marshall	1933	H.C. Smith
1927	E.A.W. Stroud	1934	H.C. Smith
1928	E.H. Bance	1935	M.O. Wells
1929	J.B. Lee	1936	C. de V. Buckingham
1930	H.C. Smith	1937	H.G. Wells
1931	D.P. Laing	1938	M.F. Hopson
1932	H. Turner	1939	Vice-Adm. D.F. Moir

Newbury & Crookham

1946	F.M. Barton	1963	A. Thomas	1980	F.H. Brown
1947	T.H. Evans	1964	R.E. Kemp	1981	A.S. Wood
1948	H. Kennedy	1965	R. Black	1982	K.J. Hanney
1949	W.K.T. Hope	1966	R. Bishop	1983	P.A. Bowles
1950	R.V.C. Wing	1967	G. Part	1984	J. Ireland
1951	W.J. Barlow	1968	J. Jolly	1985	M.J. Hounsell
1952	A.J. Swanson	1969	G. Holloway	1986	G.R. Gee
1953	P.H. Purdue	1970	W.J. Barlow	1987	J. Ireland
1954	T.H. Evans	1971	C.J. Ball	1988	L. Cummins
1955	S. Benniston	1972	P. Cronin	1989	J.J. Butler
1956	W.C. Clippendale	1973	B.A. Haskell	1990	D.R. Mavis
1957	L. Moore	1974	A.S. Daniels	1991	J. Jolly
1958	G. Holloway	1975	B.A. Haskell	1992	B.W. Bradshaw
1959	T.P.N. Greader	1976	A.W. How	1993	R.L. Swaffield
1960	A. Shirtliff	1977	B.A. Haskell	1994	R.F. Foster
1961	G.T. Blake	1978	A.S. Daniels	1995	B. Newman
1962	P.D. Clarke	1979	R.J. Marchant		

Kirby Cup

1926	S. Widdicombe	1953	R.A. Bance	1975	L.C. Pearce
1927	H.C. Smith	1954	W.J. Barlow	1976	R. Kalina
1928	H.D. Floyd	1955	A.J. Molnar	1977	D.J. Price
1929	C.B. Gilroy	1956	T.H. Whiteman	1978	D.A. Hector
1930	S. Widdicombe	1957	R. Elliott	1979	F. Fisher
1931	W. Smith	1958	T.P.N. Greader	1980	R.G. Mead
1932	C.B. Gilroy	1959	A. Shirtliff	1981	J.M. Cole
1933	Capt N.W. Tredinnick	1960	F.L. Shergold	1982	F. Boonham
1934	H.C. Smith	1961	F.N. Ball	1982	F. Boonham
1935	M.C.H. Smith-Carington	1962	R. Black	1982	F. Boonham
1936	H.G. Wells	1963	C.J. Ball	1984	J.M. Randall
1937	P.M. Barton	1964	C.J. Ball	1985	C.J. Ball
1938	P.M. Barton	1965	R. Mabbutt	1986	K. Dunks
1939	D. Thomas	1966	J.G. Miller	1987	J. Bowness
1940-45	Not played	1967	A.E. Reeves	1988	G.L. Pinder
1946	T.H. Evans	1968	B. Bowness	1989	J.S. Gilbert
1947	L. Moore	1969	J.G. Miller	1990	M. O'Shea
1948	J.N. Casserley	1970	G. Part	1991	R.J. Rodgers
1949	F.L. Shergold	1971	C. Waldeck	1992	R.D. Antmann
1950	L. Moore	1972	G.S. Wright	1993	J.A. Rhoads
1951	R. Morrison	1973	L.L. Watkins	1994	R.C. Williams
1952	F.N. Ball	1974	J.S. Fuller	1995	R.J. Mavis

Elkington Cup

Handicap Knockout

1924	H.D. Floyd	1949	R. Tull	1967	A.P. Boynton
1925	Capt Angier	1950	R.A. Bance	1968	A.P. Boynton
1926	W.K.T. Hope	1951	A.R.S. Rodford	1969	G.T. Blake
1927	W.K.T. Hope	1952	J. Whiting	1970	S.M. Wilson
1928	M.O. Wells	1953	R.A. Bance	1971	D.H. Rouse
1929	E.T. Povey	1954	C.V. Liebscher	1972	I. Walters
1930	W. Smith	1955	W.J. Barlow	1973	B.J. Bowness
1931	F.N. Ball	1956	F.A.H. Keates	1974	D. Niven
1932	A. Marshall	1957	F.N. Ball	1975	T. Howard
1933	H. Wilson	1958	G. Bowden	1976	F. Fisher
1934	J.S. Rutherford	1959	P.H. Greader	1977	R. Pierce-Williams
1935	F.M. Barton	1960	W. Howard	1978	C.J. Ball
1936	F.M. Barton	1961	L.E. Cochane	1979	S. Wood
1937	J.S. Rutherford	1962	G.W. Miller	1980	J.M. Cole
1938	S.A. Dell	1963	P.E. Risby	1981	C.J. Ball
1946	R. Tull	1964	C.J. Ball	1982	J. Niven
1947	L. Moore	1965	S. Reeh	1983	A.J. How
1948	F.M. Barton	1966	P.T. Cronin	1984	N.J. Randall

Scratch Knockout Finals (36-hole finals)

1985	R. Miles bt D. Rosier	37th		1991	B. Davies bt T. Butler	6 & 4
1986	D. Rosier			1992	T. Butler bt N. Woodage	1 up
1987	D. Rosier bt C. Ball	8 & 7		1993	K. Dunks bt N. Woodage	4 & 3
1988	J. Claridge bt J. Niven	6 & 5		1994	C.J. Ball bt J. Sandys	3 & 1
1989	T. Butler bt J. Niven	5 & 4		1995	J. G. Sandys bt J.D Axford	2 & 1
1990	H. Claxton bt J. Sandys	38th				

Ladies Scratch Championship

1972	A. Thomas	78+84=162		1983	K.L. Davies	
1973	A. Thomas	83+81=164		1984	A. Thomas	=155
1974	S. Jolly	85+81=166		1985	A. Thomas	=152
	(14 years old)			1986	G.R. Bowness	
1975	S. Jolly	80+82=162		1987	L. Arnold	
1976	A. Thomas			1988	A. Thomas	
1977	A. Thomas	77+84=161		1989	A. Thomas	81+79=160
1978	A. Thomas			1990	J. Wailes	=153
1979	J. Freemantle	=154		1991	J. WailesBV3664	
1980	L. Arnold	78+83=161		1992	A. Thomas	77+84=161
1981	K.L. Davies	76+76=152		1993	J. Wailes	74+75=149
	(after play-off with A. Thomas)			1994	D. Davies	83+83=166
1982	L. Arnold	78+78=156		1995	J. Wailes	84+80=164

Baxendale Cup

1924	Mrs Bramwell-Davis	1952	Mrs B. Simmons	1974	Mrs J. Allen
1925	Miss Plenty	1953	Lady des Voeux	1975	Mrs J. Jolly
1926	Miss Plenty	1954	Miss M. Heather	1976	Mrs R.G. Freemantle
1927	Mrs Stradling	1955	Mrs J.M. Towell	1977	Mrs M.G. Simmons
1928	Miss Stokes	1956	Miss A. Coulman	1978	Mrs D. Gourley
1929	Mrs Stow	1957	Mrs W.C. Clippingdale	1979	Mrs R.J. Key
1930	Mrs Hope	1958	Mrs P.H. Greader	1980	Mrs D. Davies
1931	Mrs Stow	1959	Mrs J.M. Towell	1981	Mrs J.E. Davies
1932	Mrs Harley	1960	Mrs D. Grahame	1982	Mrs J. Wailes
1933	Mrs D.M. Elliott	1961	Mrs L. Southern	1983	Mrs J. Wailes
1934	Mrs Hope	1962	Miss E.M. Aird	1984	Mrs J.E. Davies
1935	Miss J. Philbrick	1963	Mrs J.E.B. Dyson	1985	Mrs S.E. Swayne
1936	Mrs Priston	1964	Miss E.M. Aird	1986	Mrs J. Davies
1937	Mrs Starkey-Smith	1965	Mrs E.B. Lloyd	1987	Mrs A. Hornby
1938	Miss H.M. Dickson	1966	Miss E.M. Aird	1988	Mrs I.J. Butcher
1939-1945	Not played	1967	Mrs B.E.D. Cooper	1989	Dr L. Heitzman
1946	Mrs E.H. Bance	1968	Mrs L. Southern	1990	Mrs R.J. Key
1947	Mrs P.H. Greader	1969	Mrs E.A. Pearn	1991	Mrs J. Jolly
1948	Mrs H.I. Taylor	1970	Mrs N. McNeice	1992	Mrs G. Darby
1949	Mrs P.H. Greader	1971	Mrs J. Hamilton	1993	Mrs S. Gibbons
1950	Mrs P.H. Greader	1972	Mrs R.G. Freemantle	1994	Mrs J. Futrell
1951	Mrs E.H. Bance	1973	Mrs S. Goodall	1995	Mrs H.C. Hedger

Douglas Cup

1925	Mrs Stradling	1954	Mrs W.C. Clippingale	1975	Mrs A.P. Boynton
1926	Mrs Pellow	1955	Mrs D. Grahame	1976	Mrs A.P. Boynton
1927	Mrs Stow	1956	Miss M. Taylor	1977	Mrs A.H. Brown
1928	Miss B. Stokes	1957	Mrs D. Grahame	1978	Miss D. Millett
1929	Mrs Bance	1958	Miss E.M. Aird	1979	Mrs J. Mead
1930	Mrs Urling	1959	Mrs D. Grahame	1980	Mrs F.J. Freemantle
1931	Mrs Elliott	1960	Mrs. P.H. Greader	1981	Mrs A.P. Boynton
1932	Mrs Elliott	1961	Mrs D. Grahame	1982	Mrs G. Clifford-Smith
1933	Mrs Symonds	1962	Mrs J.M. Towell	1983	Mrs S.R. Bray
1934	Mrs Elliott	1963	Mrs D. Grahame	1984	Mrs E.M. Mackay
1935	Miss Stokes	1964	Mrs M.G. Simmonds	1985	Mrs G.R. Bowness
1936	Mrs Elliott	1965	Mrs E.S. Shotter	1986	Mrs J. Mead
1937	Miss Stokes	1966	Mrs R.E. Fletcher	1987	Mrs A.P. Boynton
1938	Mrs Elliott	1967	Mrs P.D. Clarke	1988	Mrs J. Mead
1947	Mrs Bance	1968	Mrs G. Fox	1989	Mrs S. King
1948	Mrs L. Moore	1969	Mrs G. Bradley	1990	Mrs Tim King
1949	Mrs P.H. Greader	1970	Mrs E. Howard	1991	Mrs G.R. Bowness
1950	Mrs P.H. Greader	1971	Mrs R.J. Key	1992	Mrs A. Thomas
1951	Mrs H.I. Taylor	1972	Mrs J. Jolly	1993	Lady K. Hoare
1952	Mrs B. Simmons	1973	Miss S. Jolly	1994	Mrs D.J. Davies
1953	Mrs H.I. Taylor	1974	Mrs W.F. Eastman	1995	Mrs G.R. Bowness

Platt Cup

1926	Mrs H. Stradling	1953	Mrs P.H. Greader	1975	Mrs A.H. Brown
1927	Mrs Pellow	1954	Mrs K. Huxtable	1976	Mrs J. Hamilton
1928	Miss B. Plenty	1955	Mrs H.I. Taylor	1977	Mrs J. Hamilton
1929	Mrs J.L. Stow	1956	Mrs H.W. Merckel	1978	Mrs A.D. Brown
1930	Mrs J.L. Stow	1957	Mrs D. Grahame	1979	Mrs A.K. Hathway
1931	Mrs Austin Dickson	1958	Miss M. Heather	1980	Mrs S. Hamilton
1932	Mrs Bramwell Davis	1959	Mrs E.S. Shotter	1981	Mrs G. Bowness
1933	Mrs D.M. Elliott	1960	Mrs D. Grahame	1982	Mrs V.C. Watson
1934	Miss M. Stokes	1961	Mrs P.H. Greader	1983	Mrs D.L. Davies
1935	Miss B. Dickson	1962	Mrs J.M. Towell	1984	Miss J.A. Key
1936	Miss M.E. Ball	1963	Mrs G. Fox	1985	Mrs L. Arnold
1937	Mrs D.M. Elliott	1964	Mrs H.K. Potter	1986	Mrs D.L. Davies
1938	Mrs Pellow	1965	Mrs A. Thomas	1987	Mrs B. Niven
1939	Mrs D.M. Elliott	1966	Mrs S.B. Baker	1988	Mrs B. Niven
1940	Mrs G. Cochrane	1967	Mrs P.D. Clarke	1989	Mrs J.M. Sturgess
1946	Mrs J. Whiting	1968	Mrs G. Bradley	1990	Mrs J. Goodenough
1947	Mrs E. Simmons	1969	Mrs M.G. Simmons	1991	Mrs R.F. Hall
1948	Mrs L. Moore	1970	Mrs A. Pearn	1992	Mrs J. Wailes
1949	Mrs L. Moore	1971	Mrs M.G. Simmons	1993	Mrs V. Watson
1950	Mrs H.I. Taylor	1972	Mrs R.G. Freemantle	1994	Dr D.J. Davies
1951	Mrs L. Moore	1973	Mrs A.H. Brown	1995	Mrs J. Jolly
1952	Mrs J. Whiting	1974	Mrs A. Pearn		

Philbrick Cup

1934	Mrs Elliott	1959	Miss M.K. Heather	1978	Miss D. Millett
1935	Mrs Pellow	1960	Mrs J.M. Champion	1979	Miss D. Millett
1936	Mrs Elliott	1961	Mrs F.L. Shergold	1980	Mrs A. Thomas
1937	Miss P. Saunderson	1962	Mrs P.H. Greader	1981	Mrs D.R. Gourlay
1938	Miss P. Saunderson	1963	Miss E.M. Aird	1982	Mrs L. Arnold
1939-1945 Not played		1964	Mrs A. Thomas	1983	Mrs R.J. Key
1946	Mrs. Simmons	1965	Mrs A. Thomas	1984	Mrs J. Wailes
1947	Miss M.K. Heather	1966	Mrs A. Thomas	1985	Mrs A. Thomas
1948	Mrs A. Elkington	1967	Mrs A. Thomas	1986	Mrs A. Archibald
1949	Mrs P.H. Greader	1968	Mrs A. Thomas	1987	Mrs P.C. Sinfield
1950	Mrs H.I. Taylor	1969	Mrs. A. Thomas	1988	Mrs S. Hamilton
1951	Miss M.K. Heather	1970	Mrs G.E.M. Bradley	1989	Mrs A.P. Boynton
1952	Mrs D. Grahame	1971	Mrs J. Jolly	1990	cancelled
1953	Mrs D. Grahame	1972	Mrs S. Hamilton	1991	Mrs A. Thomas
1954	Mrs D. Grahame	1973	Mrs. C.M. Longdon	1992	Mrs A. Thomas
1955	Mrs H.I. Taylor	1974	Mrs A. Thomas	1993	Mrs G. Bowness
1956	Mrs P.H. Greader	1975	Mrs C. Rolfe	1994	Mrs J. Wailes
1957	Miss A. Coulman	1976	Mrs A.P. Boynton	1995	Mrs N. Kirby
1958	Mrs D. Grahame	1977	Mrs R.J. Key		

Stokes Salver

1937	Miss H. Dickson	1960	Mrs P.H. Greader	1978	Miss D. Millett
1938	Mrs D.M. Elliott	1961	Mrs A. Thomas	1979	Mrs R.G. Freemantle
1939	Mrs B. Cochrane	1962	Mrs A. Thomas	1980	Mrs R.J. Key
1940	Mrs K. Huxtable	1963	Mrs A. Thomas	1981	Mrs G. Bowness
1946	Mrs J. Whiting	1964	Mrs J.M. Towell	1982	Mrs L. Heitzman
1947	Mrs J. Whiting	1965	Mrs A. Thomas	1983	Mrs E. Longden
1948	Mrs A. Elkington	1966	Mrs S.B. Baker	1984	Mrs G. Bowness
1949	Mrs K. Huxtable	1967	Mrs B.E.D. Cooper	1985	Mrs D.R. Gourlay
1950	Mrs P.H. Greader	1968	Mrs A. Thomas	1986	Mrs L. Arnold
1951	Miss A. Moore	1969	Mrs P.D. Clarke	1987	Mrs S.M. Claxton
1952	Miss A. Moore	1970	Mrs A. Thomas	1988	Mrs R. Shaw
1953	Miss A. Moore	1971	Mrs E. Howard	1989	Mrs D.R. Gourlay
1954	Miss M. Heather	1972	Mrs A. Thomas	1990	Mrs S.H. Jordan
1955	Miss A. Moore	1973	Mrs R.J. Key	1991	Mrs J. Wailes
1956	Mrs J. Whiting	1974	Miss D. Hall-Wilton	1992	Mrs E.A. Dunks
1957	Miss M. Heather	1975	Mrs R.G. Freemantle	1993	Mrs S.M. Claxton
1958	Mrs D. Grahame	1976	Mrs J. Jolly	1994	Mrs D.J. Davies
1959	Mrs P.H. Greader	1977	Miss D. Millett	1995	Mrs G.R. Bowness

Newbury Racecourse

Newbury and Crookham

Site of The Voluntee